TYPES
IN
HEBREWS

TYPES IN HEBREWS

SIR ROBERT ANDERSON

Kregel
Classics

Types in Hebrews by Sir Robert Anderson. © 1978 by Kregel
Publications, a division of Kregel, Inc., P.O. Box 2607, Grand
Rapids, MI 49501. All rights reserved. First Kregel Publica-
tions edition: 1978.

Library of Congress Cataloging-in-Publication Data
Anderson, Robert, Sir, 1841–1918.
   Types in Hebrews.

   (Sir Robert Anderson library)
   Reprint of the 2nd ed. published by Pickering & Inglis,
London, under title: The Hebrews Epistle in the light of
the types.
   Includes index.
      1. Bible, N. T. Hebrews—Criticism, interpretation, etc.
2. Typology (Theology) I. Title. II. Series: Anderson, Rob-
ert, Sir. 1841–1918. Sir Robert Anderson Library.
BS2775.A53   1978   227'.87'06   78-9545
                                                    CIP

ISBN 978-0-8254-2577-6

1 2 3 4 5 / 12 11 10 09 08
Printed in the United States of America

CONTENTS

CONTENTS

Preface

PREFACE

The elucidation of the doctrine of the types, now entirely neglected, is an important problem for future theologians. If Hengstenberg were alive today we would find reason to change the adverb in this sentence. Still there is much to be done if theology is to be cleared from the accusation that the study of Scriptural typology is neglected.

The following pages are just a small contribution to the many books now available on this subject. This book is not a commentary on the Book of Hebrews. Its sole aim is to bring the light of the Old Testament types to bear on the main teachings of the Hebrews epistle and on certain passages which are often misinterpreted.

Hebrews has a very special voice for us in the " trials of our own times," as Bishop Westcott mentions in his commentary. Those who take the skeptic's view of the Old Testament, primarily the Pentateuch, are joining the long line of individuals who are cheating themselves of the blessing of having the proper ammunition to fight the spiritual battles that are part of our everyday lives. An effort is made herein to give a prominent place to the teachings of the Hebrews epistle, so that we may have the proper understanding of the types of the Old Testament and their application to the Christian life.

Hebrews is misread by those who fail to recognize that the Christian revelation is based on the fact that God also is the originator of Judaism. To borrow a phrase from Lord Beaconsfield, the Hebrew Christian is "a completed Jew", and it was in this character that the Apostle Paul always addressed himself to his "kinsmen after the flesh." It is this fact that has cleared my own mind of all doubt that the Apostle Paul is the real author of the Book of Hebrews.

The Publishers

TYPES IN HEBREWS

1

AUTHORSHIP

THE authorship of Hebrews has been a subject of controversy during all the centuries. Was it written by the Apostle whose name it bears in our English Bibles? Or does the honour rest with Luke the Evangelist? The claims of Barnabas and Apollos, and also of Clement of Rome, are championed by writers of eminence. There is a venerable tradition that the Epistle was written in Hebrew by the Apostle, and that our Greek version is the work of the Evangelist. And our only difficulty in accepting that tradition is the absence of evidence to support it. As for the other companions of the Apostle, their claims rest on mere conjecture; there is not a scintilla of *evidence* to connect them with the book. And the question at issue is purely one of evidence. It must be settled on the principles which govern the decisions of our Courts of Justice. As therefore the evidence which points to Luke as the writer is unquestionably inferior to that available in support of the Pauline authorship, the controversy might be closed at once were it not for certain difficulties suggested by the language and contents of the Epistle.

It has literary characteristics, we are told, different from those which mark the well-known writings of the Apostle. "The Judaism of the Epistle is that of the Hebrew prophets," and not of the Pharisees. And lastly, the writer takes his place among those who received the revelation of the Messiah mediately through "them that heard Him," whereas the Apostle Paul maintained with emphasis that he received the gospel immediately from the Lord Himself. This is held to be a "fatal" objection to the Pauline authorship. But, as every one who has had much experience in dealing with evidence is aware, a solution may often be found of difficulties and objections which at first seem "fatal"; and the sequel will show perhaps that the Hebrews controversy is a case in point. The difficulties suggested by the language of the book shall be considered later.

Even from the earliest times the Roman Church has viewed Hebrews with suspicion. And the reason for this is not doubtful. It is amply accounted for by the fact that the Epistle gives such prominence to the covenant people, and that its teaching is utterly incompatible with the proud ecclesiastical pretensions which, even from the days of the Fathers, that church has championed. The following extract from Dr. Hatch's *Bampton Lectures* may explain my meaning:

" In the years of transition from the ancient to the modern world, when all civilised society seemed to be disintegrated, the confederation of the Christian churches, by the very fact of its existence upon the old imperial lines, was not only the most powerful, but the only powerful organisation in the civilised world. It was so vast and powerful, that it seemed to be, and there were few to question its being, the visible realisation of that Kingdom of God which our Lord Himself had preached, of that ' Church ' which He had purchased with His own blood. . . . This confederation was the ' city of God '; this and no other was the ' Holy Catholic Church.' "

The error denounced in these eloquent words betrays ignorance not only of Christian truth, but of what may be described as the ground-plan of the Biblical revelation as a whole. And yet the beliefs even of spiritual Christians are leavened by it. In laying the foundation stone of a great building it is a common practice to bury documents relating to the scheme and purpose of the edifice. And concealed in the foundations of the self-styled " Holy Catholic Church " (how different is the meaning given to these words by the Reformers!) is the flagrant falsehood that God has finally cast away the people of the covenant. To the history and hopes and destiny of that people it is that, on its human side, the Bible mainly and primarily relates; and yet the only notice accorded to them by the two great rival branches of the apostasy of Christendom must be sought in the records of the fiendish persecutions of which they have been the victims.

That the professing Church on earth is "the true vine"—this is the daring and impious lie of the apostasy. That it is "the olive tree" is a delusion shared by the mass of Christians in the churches of the Reformation. But the teaching of Scripture is explicit, that Christ Himself is the vine, and Israel the olive. For "God hath NOT cast away His people whom He foreknew." Most true it is that they have been temporarily set aside. Some of the natural branches of the olive tree have been broken off, and wild olive branches have been engrafted in their place. But the tree remains, and the tree is Israel.[1]

---

[1] Here, as so often in Scripture, "Israel" is used as a generic term for the people of the Abrahamic covenant. It is not a synonym for "the Jew." Though Jews had a privileged position as branches of the olive tree (Rom. xi.), *the tree* was not "the Jew," but the people of the covenant as a whole ; and "the root and fatness" of which we Gentiles partake, points, not to Judaism, but right back to Abraham.

But the very same Scripture which records this, declares explicitly that the wild branches which, " contrary to nature," "" partake of the root and fatness of the olive tree," are liable to be themselves " broken off," and then the natural branches will be again restored.

While, therefore, the apostate Church claims to be the realisation of God's supreme purpose for earth, the intelligent student of Scripture knows that even in its pristine purity the " Gentile Church " was an abnormal, episodical, temporary provision ; and that the divine purpose for this age is to gather out the true and heavenly Church, the body of Christ ; and then, dismissing the earthly church to its predicted doom, to restore to their normal position of privilege and blessing that chosen people to whom belong the adoption and the glory and the covenants, and the giving of the law, and the service of God, and the promises ; whose are the fathers, and of whom is Christ as concerning the flesh.[1]

That these inspired words of the Apostle are no mere reference to a past economy, but a statement of abiding truth, is made definitely clear by the sequel ending with the words : " For the gifts and calling of God are without repent-

[1] Rom. ix. 4, 5.

ance." [1]   And it is truth which may help not only to a right understanding of the Epistle to the Hebrews, but incidentally to the solution of the problem of its authorship.

---

[1] Rom. xi. 29. The seeming contradiction between verse 15 and verses 1 and 2 is due to the same English word being used to translate two different words in the original.

It may be well to notice here once again, for it is often ignored, that "Israel" is not a synonym for "the Jew." This appears in a very marked way in Romans. In the first section of that Epistle, where the Apostle is dealing with the nation then in evidence, in relation to their blessings and responsibilities with respect to Christ and the Gospel, it is only and always "the Jew." But after ch. iii. 1 the Jew is never expressly named again save in ix. 24 and x. 12, where he refers parenthetically to his opening theme. "Israel," on the other hand, is never mentioned until chapters ix., x., and xi. And in those three chapters the word occurs twelve times. For there the Apostle is dealing with the past and the future; and therefore he has in view "the seed of Abraham" in a fuller and wider sense.

2

OTHER TESTIMONY

"God, having of old time spoken unto the fathers in the prophets . . . spake unto us in His Son."

Does the "us" here refer to us Christians of the Gentile dispensation? The question is not whether the Epistle has a voice for us; "Every student of Hebrews must feel that it deals in a peculiar degree with the thoughts and trials of our own time,"[1] but what was the meaning which they to whom it was primarily addressed were intended to put upon the words? The opening verses are an undivided sentence; and as "the fathers" were Israel, we may assume with confidence that the "us" must be similarly construed.

There was no "us" in the Apostle Paul's references to the revelation with which he was entrusted as Apostle to the Gentiles. "My Gospel" he calls it. And again, "that Gospel which I preach among the Gentiles." It was the precious charge, "the good deposit"[2] which, in view of his passing from his labours to his

---

[1] Bishop Westcott.　　[2] The *kalē parathēkē* (2 Tim. i. 14).

rest, he very specially committed to his most
trusted fellow-worker. But much as he "mag-
nified his office" as Apostle to the Gentiles,
he never forgot, and never ceased to boast,
that he was an Israelite. And he had a special
ministry to the covenant people. To them it
was that he first addressed himself in every
place he visited throughout the whole circuit of
his recorded labours.[1] Even in Rome, although
his relations with the Christians there were so
close and so tender, his first care was to call
together "the chief of the Jews."

And, assuming the Pauline authorship of
Hebrews, the book was the work, not of "the
Apostle to the Gentiles," but of Paul the
Messianic witness to Israel — "our beloved
brother Paul," as "the Apostle to the Circumcision" designates him with reference (*ex
hypothesi*) to this very Epistle.

This lends a special significance to the tense
of the verbs in the opening sentence. "God,
having spoken to the fathers in the prophets,
spake to us in the Son." In the one case as in
the other the reference is to a past and completed
revelation. It is not the distinctively Christian

---

[1] This is all the more remarkable because his ministry during the
interval between his first and last Roman imprisonments is not recorded.
It must have been of peculiar interest and importance, but it was outside the scope of Scripture. It is not accidental, but the result of a
divine purpose, that the book of the Acts ends where it does.

revelation which was still in course of promulgation in the Epistles to Gentile churches, but the revelation of the Messiah in His earthly ministry —that ministry in respect of which He Himself declared "I am not sent but to the lost sheep of the House of Israel." For, as the inspired Apostle wrote, "Christ was *a minister of the circumcision* for the truth of God to confirm the promises made unto the fathers, and that the Gentiles might glorify God for His mercy."[1] *Promises* for Israel, but *mercy* for those who were "strangers to the covenants of promise."[2]

These words may remind us of the distinction already noticed between the Judaism of the Hebrew Scriptures, and the Judaism of the Pharisees. Using the word "religion" in its classical acceptation, the religion of the Pentateuch is the only divine religion the world has ever known; for in that sense Christianity is not a religion, but a revelation and a faith. The little company of spiritual Israelites who became the first disciples of Christ accepted Him because He was the realisation and fulfilment of that divine religion. But the religion of the nominal Jew was as false as is the religion of the nominal Christian. And while "the Jews' religion," which rejected Christ, is denounced in the Apostle Paul's ministry toward

---

[1] Rom. xv. 8, 9.   [2] Eph. ii. 12.

Judaisers, the divine religion which pointed to Christ is unfolded in the Epistle to the Hebrews.

" That gospel which I preach among the Gentiles." These words are usually read with a false emphasis. It is not " the gospel which *I* preach,"[1] as contrasted with the preaching of the other Apostles, but " the gospel which I preach *among the Gentiles*," as contrasted with his own preaching to Israel. And the contrast will be clear to any one who will compare his epistles to Gentile churches with his sermon to the Jews of Antioch in Pisidia.[2] There was not a word in that sermon which might not have been spoken by any Jew who had embraced the faith of Christ at or after Pentecost. It is based entirely on the history, and the promises and hopes, of Israel, and upon the coming and work of Christ as recorded in the Gospels—the salvation, as Hebrews expresses it, " confirmed unto us by them that heard Him." Writing as an Israelite to Israelites, the words of Hebrews ii. 2 are just what we should expect from the Apostle Paul. They are the precise counterpart of his words recorded in Acts xiii. 26, 33. And if the one passage be proof that he could not have been the author of Hebrews, the other is equal proof

---

[1] There is no *ego* in the Greek.   [2] Acts xiii. 16–41.

that he could not have been the preacher at Antioch.[1]

We thus see that what appeared to be a fatal bar to the Pauline authorship of Hebrews admits of a solution which is both simple and adequate. And we can understand why the Apostle did not declare himself in the opening words, according to his usual practice. For the writer, I again repeat, was not "the Apostle to the Gentiles," but Paul "of the stock of Israel," "a Hebrew of the Hebrews." To describe the book as "anonymous" is a sheer blunder; for the concluding chapter gives the clearest proof that the writer was well known to those whom he was addressing.

Due weight has never been given to this fact in estimating the value of the general testimony of the Greek Fathers that the writer was the Apostle Paul. To attribute equal value to the statements of certain Latin Fathers of a later date betrays ignorance of the science of evidence. The testimony of the earlier Fathers, moreover, is confirmed in the most striking way by the explicit statement of 2 Peter iii. 15, that Paul did in fact write an Epistle to Hebrews. And if this be not that Epistle, what and where can it be?

[1] Stuart's book on *Hebrews* refers to a suggestion of Berger that this Antioch sermon was the basis of the Epistle.

But this is not all. Writers without number have noticed the striking fact that the book is a treatise rather than an epistle. This is met, however, by pointing to the strictly epistolary character of the closing chapter. But may not the twenty-second verse of that chapter afford the solution of this seeming paradox? "Bear with the word of exhortation, for I have written unto you in few words."[1] Apart from the authorship controversy no one would venture to suggest that this could refer to the book as a whole. Even in these days of typewriters, such an ending to a letter of some 8000 words would be worthy of a silly schoolgirl! To common men the suggestion will seem reasonable that chapter xiii. is "a covering letter," written to accompany the treatise. And if that letter stood alone no one but a professional sceptic would question that it emanated from the Apostle Paul. For, in every word of it, as Delitzsch so truly says, "we seem to hear St. Paul himself and no one else."

Unless therefore such a conclusion is barred on the grounds already indicated, the presumption is irresistible that the author of the letter was the author of the book. And if the solution here offered of the doctrinal pecu-

---

[1] The original is still more emphatic. It has been aptly rendered: "for it is in few words that I have written to you."

liarities of Hebrews be deemed adequate, the whole question becomes narrowed to a single issue. It is an issue, moreover, which cannot be left to the decision of Greek scholars *as such*. For even if they were agreed, which they are not, we should insist on its being considered on more general grounds. Will any student of literature maintain that so great a master of the literary art as the Apostle Paul might not, in penning a treatise such as Hebrews, display peculiarities and elegancies of style which do not appear in his epistolary writings ?

Some people might object that this remark ignores the divine inspiration of the Epistle, which is the one question of essential importance, the question of the human authorship being entirely subordinate. But if the objector's estimate of inspiration be of that kind which eliminates the element of human authorship, *cadit quæstio*. If, on the other hand, that element be recognised, it is easy to conjecture circumstances which would account for any peculiarities of style. Here, however, I should repeat, scholars differ. The following is the testimony of one of our most eminent Greek scholars: " After a study of the Greek language as diligent, and an acquaintance with its writers of every age, as extensive probably as any person at least of my own country now living, I must maintain my decided opinion that the Greek is, except as regards the *structure of sentences*, not so decidedly superior to the Greek of St. Paul as to make it even improbable that the Epistle was written by him." [1]

Any one who is accustomed to deal with the evidence of witnesses would here consider whether circumstances may not have existed to account for "the structure of sentences" in the Epistle, and for the occasional use of words not found in the Apostle's other writings. Let us suppose, for example, that Hebrews was written with "the beloved physician" by his side, either in "his own hired house" during his Roman imprisonment, [2] or in the house of some Italian Christian after his release, may he not have accepted literary suggestions from his companion? No "theory of inspiration" is adequate which does not assume Divine guidance in the very terminology of Scripture. But God makes use of means. When he fed Elijah, He used the birds of the air. And when the Lord fed the multitudes, He did not "command the stones to become bread," as the Devil suggested in the Temptation, but utilised the disciples' little store, utterly insignificant though it was. And no devout mind need refuse the

[1] Bloomfield, *Gr. Test.*, p. 465. [2] Acts xxviii. 30.

suggestion that as the Apostle read (or possibly dictated) Hebrews to his companion, the Evangelist would suggest that this sentence or that might be made more forcible by transposing its clauses, or that some other word would more fitly express the Apostle's meaning than that which he had employed.

It is, as Bengel declares, "with the general consent of antiquity" that the authorship of Hebrews is attributed to the Apostle Paul. And the only other witness I will here call is another eminent German expositor, whose great erudition is but one element in his competence to deal with this question. Franz Delitzsch's words are always weighty; but the value of his testimony to the Pauline authorship is all the greater because he ranks with those by whom the Epistle is attributed to the Evangelist. In the introduction to his Commentary he writes as follows :—

"We seem at first to have a treatise before us, but the special hortatory references interwoven with the most discursive and dogmatic portions of the work soon show us that it is really a kind of sermon addressed to some particular and well-known auditory; while at the close the homiletic form (the *Paraclesis*) changes into that of an epistle (ch. xiii. 22). The epistle has no apostolic name attached to it, while it produces throughout the impression of the presence of the original and creative force of the apostolic spirit. And if written by an Apostle, who could have been its author but St. Paul ? True, till towards the end it does not make the impression upon us of being of his authorship; its form is not Pauline, and the thoughts, though never un-Pauline, yet often go beyond the Pauline type of doctrine as made known to us in the other epistles, and even where this is not the case they seem to be peculiarly placed and applied ; but towards the close, when the epistle takes the epistolary form, we seem to hear St. Paul himself, and no one else." [1]

---

[1] I add the following from *The Speaker's Commentary*. "The question then is this: shall the positive testimony of men who, knowing St. Paul intimately, were qualified to give witness on such a point, be outweighed by the doubts of those who lived some hundred years later, and therefore were not so qualified " (p. 5).

3

HEBREWS IN THE OLD TESTAMENT

"GOD, having of old time spoken unto the fathers in the prophets by divers portions and in divers manners, hath at the end of these days spoken unto us in His Son."[1]

Thus the Epistle to the Hebrews opens by declaring the divine authority of the Old Testament Scriptures. It is not merely that they were written by holy and gifted men, but that they are a divine revelation. God spoke in the prophets. And the mention of "prophets" must not lead us to limit the reference to what we call "the prophetic Scriptures." Both in Hebrew and in Greek the term used is wide enough to include all the "divers manners" in which God spoke to men—not only by prophecy (as the term is commonly understood), but by promise, law, exhortation, warning, type, parable, history. And always through individual men specially chosen and accredited. Through them it was that the revelation came. The highest privilege of "the Jewish Church" was

---

[1] Still more literally the passage reads: "In many parts and in many ways, of old, God having spoken to the fathers in the prophets in these last days spake to us in (His) Son."

its being entrusted with these "oracles of God";
for not even in its darkest days did that church
pretend to be itself the oracle. But the Christian
apostasy is marked by a depth of blindness and
profanity of which the Jew was incapable.

To understand this Epistle we need to be
familiar with the language in which it is written.
And it is the language of that "divine kindergarten"—the typology of the Pentateuch. The
precise point in Israel's typical history at which
the Epistle opens is the 24th chapter of Exodus;
and this gives us the key to its scope and purpose. The Israelites were slaves in Egypt, but
more than this, they had fallen under Egypt's
doom. For the death sentence was not upon
the Egyptians only, but upon all the inhabitants
of the land.[1]

But God not only provided a redemption, He
also delivered His people from the House of
Bondage. They were redeemed *in* Egypt by the
blood of the Passover, and they were brought out
of Egypt "with a mighty hand and with an out-
stretched arm."[2] And standing on the wilderness shore of the sea, they saw the waters closing
over their enemies, and raised their triumph song
to their Saviour God.[3] But not even deliverance
from both the guilt and the slavery of sin can

---

[1] "All the first-born in the land of Egypt shall die" (Exod. xi. 5);
the first-born here, as usually, representing the family.

[2] Deut. xxvi. 8.   [3] Exod. xv.

give either title or fitness to draw near to a holy God. And at Sinai His care was lest the people, although thus redeemed, should approach the mountain on which He was about to display His glory.[1]

The twenty-fourth chapter of Exodus emphasises this still more strongly; for there we read that even Aaron and the elders were excluded. Moses alone might come near. And Moses' right of access was due to his being a type of Christ, as mediator of the covenant. The record then recounts the dedication of the covenant. The blood of the covenant sacrifices was sprinkled on the people—the elders presumably representing the whole congregation of Israel— and *then* we read, Aaron and the elders ascended the mountain along with Moses. But yesterday it would have been death to them to " break through to gaze." But now " they saw God." And such was their " boldness," due to the blood of the covenant, that " they did eat and drink " in the divine presence.

The man of the world will ask, How could " the blood of calves and goats " make any difference in their fitness to approach God ? And the answer is, Just in the same way that a few pieces of paper may raise a pauper from poverty to wealth. The bank-note paper is

---

[1] Exod. xix. 21.

intrinsically worthless, but it represents gold in the coffers of the Bank of England. Just as valueless was that "blood of slain beasts," but it represented "the precious blood of Christ." And just as in a single day the bank-notes may raise the recipient from pauperism to affluence, so that blood availed to constitute the Israelites a holy people in covenant with God.

What was the next step in the typical story of redemption? By the sprinkling of the blood of the covenant Israel was sanctified; and then, to the very people who were warned against daring to draw near to God, the command was given, "Let them make Me a sanctuary *that I may dwell among them.*"[1] Moses, the mediator of the covenant, having thus made purification of the sins of the people, went up to God. This was the type, the shadow, of which we have in Hebrews the fulfilment, the reality; for when the Son of God "had made purification of sins" "by the blood of the everlasting covenant," he went up to God, and "sat down on the right hand of the Majesty on high."[2]

Here, then, it is that Hebrews takes up the story of redemption. Not at the twelfth chapter of Exodus, but at the twenty-fourth. The

---

[1] Exod. xxv. 8. [2] Heb. i. 3; *cf.* xiii. 20.

Passover has no place in the doctrine of the Epistle. Its purpose is to teach how sinners, redeemed from both the penalty and the bondage of sin, and brought into covenant relationship with God, can be kept on their wilderness way as "holy brethren, partakers of a heavenly calling."[1]

Such a great redemption implies a great Redeemer; and His divine glory is the theme of the opening section of the book. A superstitious assent to the dogma of His Deity is so common in Christendom that we need to be reminded that a real heart belief of that supreme truth is the mark of divine spiritual enlightenment. And we utterly fail to realise the depth of meaning, the almost dramatic force, which the Old Testament Scriptures here cited would have with a godly Jew. Let any one read a Jewish commentary on the forty-fifth Psalm, for example, and then try to gauge the thoughts of a Hebrew saint on learning that the words of the sixth verse of that Psalm are divinely addressed to Him whom the nation called the crucified blasphemer! "Thy throne, O God, is for ever and ever." Every element of prejudice and superstition which leads a nominal Christian to accept this would make the true Hebrew realise his need of divine

---

[1] Chap. iii. 1.

grace to enable him to assent to it and to grasp its meaning.

And yet the great truth which is thus enforced by quotations from the Hebrew Scriptures is implicitly asserted in the opening sentence of the Epistle. " God spake to us in His Son." To a Gentile this may have but little meaning —how little may be judged by the Revisers' marginal note ;[1] for we are accustomed to hear that we are all sons of God, and that " Jesus is our elder brother." But the Lord's claim to be Son of God was rightly understood by the Jews to be an explicit claim to Deity ; and because of it they decreed His death.[2]

And that claim is stated here with new emphasis. Our English idiom will not permit of our reproducing precisely the words of the text, and yet we can appreciate their vivid and telling force : " To us God spoke in Son."

---

[1] The marginal note in R.V. is " Gr., *a Son*." What can this mean ? It cannot be intended to delude the ignorant multitude into supposing that the Greek text has the indefinite article ! Nor yet that the absence of the Greek article requires the indefinite article in English. (When the word " Christ " is anarthrous, are we to read " a Christ " ? Must John i. 1 be rendered " the Word was with the God, and the Word was a God " ?) We dare not dismiss the note as merely thoughtless pedantry ; but the only alternative left is that it is meant to suggest a Unitarian exegesis. And yet the painful suspicion receives colour from the R.V. rendering of chap. v. 8, and vii. 28. Here we turn with a feeling of relief to Bishop Westcott's gloss, " God spake to us in one who has this character that He is Son."

[2] John v. 18 ; x. 33, 36. As regards the significance of the title as connoting Deity, I venture to refer to my book, *The Lord from Heaven.* Published by Kregel Publications, 1978.

The Hebrew Scriptures are divine, for they were given through men who "spake as they were moved by the Holy Spirit," but the words of Christ have a still higher dignity, for He Himself is God.

But to some this truth that He is God may seem to create an impassable gulf between the redeemed and the Redeemer. For we are but men—weak and sinful men, who need not only mercy and help, but sympathy. But there is no such gulf. For though He is "the effulgence of the glory (of God) and the very image of His substance," and upholds all things by the word of His power, He came down to earth, to take part of flesh and blood, to live as a man among men, and to die a shameful death at the hands of men. And having thus been "made perfect through suffering," He has become "a merciful and faithful High-priest in things pertaining to God."[1]

And yet we must not overlook the special setting in which this wonderful truth is here revealed. The Apostle Paul was divinely commissioned to unfold the great characteristic truths of Christianity—"grace, salvation-bringing to all men," and Christ "a ransom for all." But they must have a strange conception of what inspiration means, who can cavil

---

[1] See p. 65, *post.*

because these truths have no place in Hebrews. For here we have to do, not with the children of Adam, but with "the children of Abraham," who is the father of all believers. Nor are we told how lost sinners can be saved, but how saved sinners on their way to rest can be "made perfect in every good work to do His will."

The glorious truth of the love of God to a lost world must not be limited by the teaching of Hebrews, neither must the truth revealed in Hebrews be frittered away by ignoring its special meaning. In a sense the Lord has taken up the seed of Adam, but not in the sense in which, Hebrews tells us, " He taketh hold of the seed of Abraham." For though God loves the world, He loves His own the best; and "the children " in Hebrews are not the Adamic race, but the children of the promise, the children of God. And these, and these alone, it is that the Lord here calls His brethren.[1]

---

[1] I cannot allow my appreciation of Bishop Westcott's book on Hebrews to prevent my dissenting emphatically from his teaching here. Leaning, as he does, to the heresies of certain of the Greek Fathers on the subject of the Incarnation, he calls it " the foundation of Christ's High-priesthood " (p. 70). And on p. 189 he speaks of a new covenant between God and man, established by the Incarnation; and of "Jesus—the Son of Man—being entered into the presence of God *for men*." And again, "Jesus, the Son of Man, has been exalted . . . as Priest."

But whether we study the types of the Pentateuch or the teaching of Hebrews, nothing can be clearer than that the new covenant depends, not upon the birth of Christ, but upon His death. And

Many a Scripture may be studied in the market-place, but we must withdraw from the market-place to the sanctuary if we are to join in the worship, or profit by the teaching, of the Epistle to the Hebrews.

---

it is a covenant established absolutely for the redeemed, and not "between God and man" (see p. 56, *post*). And Hebrews teaches most emphatically that it is not as man, but as the Son of God, that Christ is High-priest (see pp. 30, 31, *post*). And moreover His title of Son of Man is neither derived from, nor dependent upon, the Incarnation. It is a heavenly title, connoting a heavenly glory. As Son of Man He "descended out of heaven" (John iii. 13). The Christian who has learned to note the hidden harmony of Scripture will here recall the language of Gen. i. 26, "Let us make man in our image, after our likeness." "The type," as the biologist would say, is not the creature of Eden, but He after whose likeness the creature was fashioned. (These last sentences are quoted from the author's book, *The Lord from Heaven*, to which he begs to refer for a full statement of this great truth.)

4

PRIESTHOOD

" WHEREFORE, holy brethren, partakers of a heavenly calling, consider the Apostle and High-priest of our profession, Christ Jesus."

It was the divine intention that the offices of Apostle and High-priest in Israel should be united; but, yielding to the entreaties of Moses, God permitted Aaron to share the ministry.[1] Save for this, however, the type had its exact fulfilment. For not until the mediator of the covenant had "made purification of sins," and had gone up the mount to God, was Aaron appointed high-priest; and not until the Son of God had completed the work of redemption, and ascended to the right hand of the Majesty on high, was He called[2] of God High-priest after the order of Melchisedek.

It is not that the Lord then entered upon high-priestly functions of a new character, but that, while on earth (as the Apostle expressly

---

[1] Exod. iv. 14.
[2] Heb. v. 10. Etymologically the word here rendered "call" refers to the market-place, *i.e.* it suggests a public announcement. Grimm's *Lexicon* gives it " to accost, salute; to give a name to publicly."

declares),[1] " He *would not be a priest at all.*"
And on earth it was that His *sacrificial* work
in redemption was accomplished. That work,
therefore, must have been complete before He
entered on His High-priestly office.

Repetition may be pardoned here, for our
minds are leavened by the pagan conception of
priesthood which prevails in Christendom, by
which these vital truths of Christianity are
secretly undermined or openly denied. By the
blood of the paschal lamb the Israelites were
redeemed *in Egypt,* in all the hopelessness and
degradation of their doom and their bondage.
They were then delivered *out of Egypt,* and
permitted to see the destruction of the power
that had enslaved them. And finally, by the
blood of the covenant, they became a holy
people, and gained the right to approach their
Jehovah God. And all this before Aaron was
appointed to the priestly office. " Now these
things happened unto them by way of example,
and they were written for our admonition." [2]
God saves the sinner *in his sins,* as he is and
where he is; He saves him also *from his sins,*
and teaches him that sin has no longer the
power to enslave him. Not only so, but the

---

[1] Chap. viii. 4. R.V. To apply these words to Christ as exalted
and glorified is surely a transparent error. If He now deigned to
serve on earth no such limitation could possibly apply.

[2] 1 Cor. x. 11.

sinner is sanctified by the blood of the covenant, and accorded the right of access to God.[1] And all this, both in the type and the antitype, without the intervention of priesthood. The priest was appointed in Israel to maintain the people in the enjoyment of the blessings thus secured to them by redemption. And his duties were of such a character that the humblest Israelite could have discharged them, had not God decreed that none but sons of Aaron should hold the office.

In contradistinction to all this, the pagan priest bars approach to the shrine, and claims to be endowed with mystical powers which enable him to dispense to his dupes the benefits his god is willing to bestow. And the so-called Christian priest, not being a son of Aaron, must of course be of the pagan order; and he naturally displays that veritable hall-mark of paganism, a claim to mystical powers. "A Christian priest"! Save in respect of the spiritual priesthood of all the "holy brethren," a man might as well call himself a Christian infidel,[2] for the whole position denies the perfectness and sufficiency both of the redeeming work of the Lord Jesus Christ before His ascension, and of His

---

[1] Heb. x. 29.

[2] I am not referring to the Reformers' use of the word priest as a synonym for "presbyter"—one of their efforts toward compromise, which are used with such unscrupulousness to-day.

atoning work in heaven for His people now. As
Bishop Lightfoot declares, "The only priests
under the Gospel are the saints, the members of
the Christian brotherhood." [1]

That the priesthood of Christ could not be
Aaronic, the Apostle impresses on the Jewish
mind by pointing to the fact that "our Lord
sprang out of Judah, of which tribe Moses spake
nothing concerning priesthood." And the truth
in question is made "still more evident," he
adds, by the fact that the Lord's priesthood
was divinely declared to be of the order of
Melchisedek. That Melchisedek was a type of
the Messiah the Jews themselves admitted; and
his priesthood had to do, not with offering
sacrifices for sins, but with ministering blessing
and succour and sustenance. And with the
Jew no further proof of his transcendent great-
ness was needed than the fact that "even the
Patriarch Abraham" paid him homage, giving
him "tithes of the chief spoils." [2]

The language used of him is full of mystery.
"Priest of the most high God"—a title of the
Supreme as Lord of heaven and earth—"king
of righteousness"; "king of peace"; "without
father, without mother, without genealogy, having neither beginning of days nor end of life, but
made like unto the Son of God." [3] Whatever

---

[1] See p. 77, *post.*   [2] Chap. vii. 4.   [3] Chap. vii. 2, 3.

meaning may be placed upon these words with reference to the type, it is certain that their application to Christ is meant to teach that it is as Son of God that He is High-priest.

This truth rings out loud and clear at the end of chapter iv., which tells us that we have " a great High-priest who hath passed through the heavens, Jesus *the Son of God.*" And then at the beginning of chapter v., by way of " tacit comparison with Christ, the *divine* High-priest," the Apostle goes on to speak of priests " taken from among men." [1]

And yet the Revisers have adopted a rendering of the opening words of chapter v., which make them seem to the English reader to contradict the clear and emphatic teaching of the Epistle. The Apostle's statement is explicit, that " Every high-priest taken *from among men* is appointed . . . that he may offer gifts and sacrifices for sins." [2] But, instead of this, the R.V. tells us that " Every high-priest, being taken from among men," is appointed for this purpose. The following will illustrate the difference between the text and this perversion of it. A military handbook reads : " Every commissioned officer taken from the ranks is appointed for special merit." But

---

[1] Bloomfield (*Greek Test.*). Bengel's note is " an antithesis to Christ; for the Apostle is speaking of the Levitical priesthood." In the original the words " from among men " are emphatic.

[2] Compare viii. 3, where " for sins " is omitted.

some editor changes this to " *Every commissioned officer, being taken from the ranks, is appointed for special merit.*" The " reviser " thus attributes to the author two statements, both of which are false. For every commissioned officer is *not* raised from the ranks, neither is he appointed for special merit. And so here, Hebrews teaches explicitly and with emphasis, first, that in contrast with the Aaronic high-priests who were taken from among men, our great High-priest is *Son of God.* And secondly, that, as High-priest, He has nothing to do with offering sacrifices for sins : for ere He ascended, and entered on His High-priestly office, He offered the one great sin-offering that has for ever put away sins.

Hence the change of attitude mentioned so emphatically in chapter x. 11, 12. The Aaronic priest was ever *standing*, for his work was never done ; " But HE, when He had offered one sacrifice for sins for ever, *sat down* on the right hand of God." [1]

This may lead us to notice the distinction between functions which are essential to priesthood, and those which were peculiar to priests of the Aaronic order. As we have already seen, Scripture lends no sanction to the prevailing belief that a sacrifice is essentially a priestly rite.

[1] Chap. x. 11, 12.

If, as we know, the *entire* ritual of the day of Atonement devolved upon Aaron, this was not only because the yearly sin-offering was for the whole congregation of Israel,[1] but because his acts were in a peculiar sense typical of the work of Christ. The Aaronic high-priest therefore was appointed to offer sacrifices for sin (Heb. v. 1); but neither offering nor killing the ordinary sin-offering was the work of the priest, but of the sinner who had sinned. The words of the law are explicit: "He shall lay his hand upon the head of the goat, and kill it in the place where they kill the burnt-offering before the Lord: it is a sin-offering."[2]

Not until the sacrifice had been offered, the victim slain, the blood shed, did priestly work begin. Very strikingly does this appear in the ritual prescribed for a sin committed by the whole congregation. Though, of course, the priests were implicated in a *national* sin, it was not the sons of Aaron who offered the sin-offering, but the elders of the congregation. And the elders it was who laid their hands upon the victim's head and proceeded to kill it.[3]

---

[1] Mark the words of chap. ix. 7, "for himself." And of course if the special sin was committed by the priest, he himself was responsible for the whole ritual. Lev. iv. 3 f.

[2] Lev. iv. 24, 29, 33.   [3] Lev. iv. 13 ff.

For "offer" is not a synonym for "kill." [1]
When the Apostle Paul spoke of "the offering
up of the Gentiles," [2] he was not contemplating
a holocaust of the converts! His use of the
term in this passage should safeguard us against
the common misreading of his words that Christ
"offered Himself" to God. The study of Scripture typology will save us from that extra-
ordinary vagary of Gentile exegesis that this
refers to Calvary, and that the Lord officiated as
a priest at His own death.

Here are the opening words of the Book
of Leviticus. "And the Lord called unto
Moses, and spake unto him out of the tabernacle of the congregation, saying, Speak unto
the children of Israel, and say unto them, If
any man of you bring an offering unto the
Lord . . . he shall offer it of his own voluntary
will at the door of the tabernacle of the congregation before the Lord. And he shall put
his hand upon the head of the burnt-offering,
and it shall be accepted for him to make atonement for him. And he shall kill the bullock
before the Lord : and the priests, Aaron's
sons, shall bring the blood, and sprinkle the

---

[1] This statement is not invalidated by the fact that one of the nine
Hebrew words translated "offer" in A.V. does sometimes mean "kill."
See *ex. gr.*, Lev. xvii. 5, 7.

[2] Rom. xv. 16. The marginal note "sacrificing" might perhaps
mislead the uninstructed.

blood round about upon the altar that is by the door of the tabernacle of the congregation."[1] The fact that in this passage " offer " and " bring " represent the same Hebrew verb might guard us from the error of supposing that any sacerdotal meaning is inherent in the former term.[2] The Israelite offered (or presented) his sacrifice at the door of the tabernacle, and if found to be according to the law it was accepted. He then killed the victim, having first identified himself with it by laying his hands upon its head. And the sacrificial work being thus completed, " the priests, Aaron's sons," proceeded to execute their peculiar priestly functions in making atonement for the offerer.

This ritual will enable us to understand those wonderful words already quoted, that Christ " offered Himself without spot to God." [3] This was not at the Cross, but when, " *on coming into the world*," He said, " Lo, I come to do Thy will, O God." [4] As the result, the divine will led Him to His death of shame. But neither

---

[1] Lev. i. 1–5. The kindred ritual for the sin-offering is given in chap. iv., and for the trespass offering in chap. v.

[2] The verb *Karav*, is near of kin to *Korban* a " votive gift," used by the Lord in Mark vii. 11. It occurs frequently in Leviticus, and is variously rendered by " bring," " present," " offer," &c., and in some tenses by " approach," " draw near," &c.

[3] Chap. ix. 14. The Greek word for " without spot " is that used by the LXX. for the Hebrew term which our translators usually render " without blemish " in the Pentateuch.

[4] Chap. x. 5, 7.

His death, nor the self-surrender which led to His death, was a part of His High-priestly work. [1] Everything that was typified by the action of divinely appointed Aaronic priests " with the blood of bulls and goats," the Son of God did with His own blood when He ascended to the right hand of the Majesty on high. [2]

Until after the Exodus no sacrificing priest had ever been officially appointed; and yet throughout the preceding ages holy men had offered gifts and sacrifices. And the death of Christ was the antitype of every sacrifice, whether before or after Sinai. But in Hebrews special emphasis is laid upon the annual sin-offering of the law; and if we read the Pentateuch in the light of the Epistle, we cannot fail to see that the appointment of the high-priest, and the peculiar duties assigned to him, had special reference to the great Day of Atonement. If then God desired to teach the truth that, although the high-priest's sacrificial duties were typical of Calvary, the type would not be fulfilled by Christ in virtue of His priesthood, was it possible, in that religion of ritual and of cere-

---

[1] For it was not until His return to heaven that He entered on His High-priestly office. (See p. 26, *ante.*)

[2] And here it is that with awful profanity the sham priests of Christendom claim to intervene. Whether their pretensions be to supplement, or merely to continue, either the sacrificial or the atoning work of Christ, their profanity is infinitely greater than the sin of Korah.

monial ordinances, to teach it with greater, with more dramatic emphasis, than by commanding Aaron to divest himself of his high-priestly garments until the sacrificial rites of the day had been accomplished?

With no less definiteness does this appear in the typology of the great sin-offering of Numbers xix., which holds such an important place in the teaching of Scripture. As a rule all priestly duties which were not peculiar to Aaron could be discharged by any of his sons : why then was an exception made in this instance ? The obvious explanation is that as the type was to be fulfilled by Christ, not as High-priest, but before entering on His High-priestly office, the ritual was assigned expressly to Eleazar, *the high-priest designate*. Such is the accuracy of the types of Scripture !

Let no one feel impatient at such repeated reiteration of these most important truths; for the pagan errors which they refute are accredited by many eminent theologians. Moreover, they are in the warp and woof of the false cult of the apostasy of Christendom; and in our day they are sapping the Protestantism of our National Church.[1]

---

[1] See Appendix I , p. 157, *post.*

5

CHRIST'S DEITY ENFORCED

As already suggested, two qualifications are necessary if we are to read the Epistle to the Hebrews intelligently. We need an adequate acquaintance with the typology of Scripture, and we must understand the position and thoughts of the Hebrew Christians who had been led to Christ under the tutelage of the divine religion of Judaism. That Christ came to found a new religion is a figment of Gentile theology. In the classical sense of the word "religion," Judaism is the only divine religion the world has ever known; and Christ came not to destroy, but to fulfil it. As contrasted with Judaism (and in contrast also with the apostasy of Christendom), Christianity, I repeat, is not a religion,[1] but a revelation and a faith.

But the Hebrew Christians were in danger of

---

[1] "Religion *and* piety"; the great men who framed the Service-book knew the English language! In the popular sense of the word, the Scotch used to be the most religious people in the world; but when Archbishop Laud visited Scotland he was shocked to find there was no religion there—"no religion at all that I could see—which grieved me much." And in his *N. T. Synonyms*, Archbishop Trench avers, with reference to James i. 27, that Christianity is not a religion; but, to spare the feelings of his readers, he uses the Greek word!

regarding the coming of Messiah as merely an advance in a progressive revelation. God who had spoken by the prophets had now spoken in a still more authoritative way. It was a climax in the revelation, but that was all. They needed to learn that it was not merely a climax, but a crisis. For Christ was the fulfilment of the divine religion; and by the fact of His fulfilling it He abrogated it. In whole and in every part of it, that religion pointed to Him. Its mission was to prepare men for His advent, and to lead them to Him when He came. And now that He had come, any turning back to the religion was in effect a turning away from Christ.

Therefore is it that with such emphasis and elaboration Hebrews teaches us the divine glory of the Son of God, and the incomparable pre-eminence of His ministry in every aspect of it. For it is by way of contrast, rather than of comparison, that He is named, first with angels, and then with the apostle and the high-priest of the Jewish faith. Therefore is it that, in a way which to us seems laboured, the Epistle unfolds the truth that the divinely appointed shrine, with its divinely ordered ritual, and all its gorgeous furniture living and dead, were but the shadows of heavenly realities; and that, with the coming of the Son of God, the morning of shadows was past, for the light that cast them was now in the zenith of an eternal noon.

All this accounts for the many digressions by which the Apostle sought to reach the goal of his crowning exhortation in chapter x. —digressions due to prevailing ignorance and error. For in "the Judaism of the Pharisees," as in the false cult of Christendom, a priest means a *sacrificing* priest—an error which is not only antichristian, but which, as the Apostle declares in chapter v. 12, betrays ignorance of "the rudiments of the first principles of the oracles of God." And deferring for the present any fuller notice of these digressions, let us now consider the wonderful words of that exhortation. "Having therefore, brethren, boldness to enter into the holy place by the blood of Jesus, by the way which He dedicated for us, a new and living way, through the veil, that is to say, His flesh; and having a great priest over the house of God; let us draw near with a true heart in fulness of faith, having our hearts sprinkled from an evil conscience, and our bodies washed with pure water." [1]

To *come*, or *draw near*, is one of the "key words" of the Epistle. [2] It occurs first in the

[1] Heb. x. 19–22.

[2] προσέρχομαι occurs in Heb. iv. 16; vii. 25; x. 1, 22; xi. 6; and xii. 18, 22. A different word of like meaning is used in vii. 19.

exhortation of chapter iv. 16, "Having a great high-priest, . . . let us draw near with boldness unto the throne of grace." As the tense of the verb indicates, this is not an act to be done once for all, as when a sinner comes to God for salvation; it is the habit of the true Christian, who is ever conscious of his need of mercy and grace. Still more plainly does this appear in chapter vii. 25, where Christians are characteristically called "comers unto God," drawing near to Him being their normal attitude and habit. And the man of faith is similarly designated in chapter xi. 6. In the opening words of chapter x., therefore, the worshipper is described as one who thus comes or draws near. And this same word is prominent in the exhortation of the twenty-second verse.

The figurative language here employed—the blood, the veil, the sprinkled heart, the washed body—so perplexing to Gentile exegesis, would be plain and simple to the Hebrew Christian, for it is the language of the typology of that divine religion in which he had been trained.

The Israelite, as we have seen, set out upon his journey to the land of promise as one of a redeemed and holy people. But, being none the less a sinner, he was ever liable to fall; and though his sin did not put him back under

either the doom or the bondage of Egypt, it
necessarily barred his approaching the sanctuary.
His exclusion, moreover, must have been per-
manent if there had been no provision for
atonement. And if this was true in relation
to "a sanctuary of this world," how intensely
true must it be for us who have to do with
the spiritual realities of which that sanctuary
was but a shadow. Therefore is it that in the
teaching of Hebrews "to make atonement [1]
for the sins of the people" is given such
prominence in enumerating the priestly functions
of Christ.

But Hebrews teaches in part by contrast;
and whereas the Israelite had to bring a fresh
sin-offering every time he sinned ("because it
is impossible that the blood of bulls and goats
should *take away* sins"), atonement for us is
based upon the one great sacrifice which in
fact accomplished what these typical offerings
were powerless to effect. And yet, I repeat,
the need of atonement is deeper in our case
than it was with the Israelite; and were it not
for the work of our Great High-priest in the
presence of God, our sins as Christians would

---

[1] The word is ἱλάσκομαι. It occurs only here and in Luke xviii. 13; but
in the Greek Bible it represents the Hebrew verb which our translators
render "to make atonement." The death of Christ is so commonly
spoken of as the atonement that to object to this use of the word
would savour of pedantry. But in Scripture making atonement is
priestly work following and based upon a sacrificial death.

preclude our ever entering that holy presence
during all our life on earth.

If a citizen be guilty of a crime, his conviction
and sentence will dispose of the judicial question
raised by his offence; and yet if he formerly
enjoyed the right of entrée at the palace,
nothing short of a royal pardon will restore
to him that privilege. This parable may serve
to illustrate one aspect of the truth here in
question. Although the believer has vicariously
suffered the judicial consequences of his sin,
that sin would none the less bar his ever again
approaching God, were it not that by confession
and the atoning work of Christ he obtains
forgiveness.

But even though a citizen may have an
acknowledged right to appear at Court, he
may not enter the royal presence mud-splashed
or travel-soiled; and wilderness defilement, even
though contracted innocently, precluded the
Israelite from entering the sacred enclosure.
And for this also there was full provision.
But no special sin-offering was needed. The
unclean person was purged, first by being
sprinkled with "the water of purification"—
water that owed its efficacy to the great sin-
offering—and then by bathing his entire body.
The ritual is given in detail in Numbers xix.
The victim was burnt to ashes. The ashes

were preserved, and water that had flowed
over them availed to cleanse. A sin required
blood-shedding, defilement was purged by this
water (Heb. ix. 13). And, as we have seen, the
blood-shedding was the act of the man who
sinned; so here, no priest was needed; any
clean person could perform the rite (Num.
xix. 13), thus indicating that the sprinkling
and the washing are not the work of Christ
for us, but indicate our own responsibility to
seek the restoration of communion with God
by faith and repentance.

This typical ordinance of the water of purification, though ignored in our theology, fills
an important place in the teaching of Scripture.
It is the key-note of the great prophecy of
Ezekiel xxxvi., xxxvii., which loomed so large
in Jewish hopes—a prophecy Nicodemus' ignorance of which evoked the Lord's indignant
rebuke, "Art thou a teacher of Israel and knowest
not these things!"[1] "Then will I sprinkle clean
water upon you and ye shall be clean," is the
promise of the twenty-fifth verse of chapter xxxvi.,
addressed to the earthly people. But though
gathered out of all countries and brought into
their own land (verse 24), they are likened in
the next chapter to dry bones lying on the
ground. And then follows the great regenera-

---

[1] John iii. 10.

tion: "Come, O breath, and breathe upon these slain"; and the Spirit of God enters into them, and they live (verses 9, 10, 14). This is "the birth of water and the Spirit," ignorance of which on the part of a Rabbi of the Sanhedrim was as shameful as it would be for a Christian teacher not to recognise an allusion to the Nicodemus sermon. And in its application to ourselves, this is "the *loutron* of regeneration and renewing of the Holy Ghost" of Titus iii. 5.

The word "regeneration" occurs only once again in the New Testament, namely in Matthew xix. 25, where the Lord uses it with reference to the fulfilment of this very prophecy of Ezekiel xxxvi., xxxvii. And the only other mention of the *loutron* explains its symbolic meaning. I refer to Ephesians v. 26: "that He might sanctify and cleanse it (the Church) with the *loutron* of water by the word."[1] Whether it be a question of salvation for an individual sinner, or of the national regeneration of Israel, the blessing depends upon the "once for all" sacrifice of Christ, and the work of the Holy Spirit. But the great blood-shedding is past; Calvary is never to be repeated, and it is only

---

[1] The word rendered "washing" in these two passages is a noun, not a verb. The R.V. marginal note suggests a false exegesis; for *loutron* is not the Greek Bible word for "laver." In the only passage where the LXX. uses it doctrinally (Ecclesiasticus xxxi. 25), it refers to the water of purification of Numbers xix.

by the "living and eternally abiding word of God," ministered by the Holy Spirit, that sinners are born again.[1]

And as it was by recourse to the water of purification that the Israelite proved the continuing efficacy of the sin-offering to purge him from defilement, so is it with us. But we have the reality of which the water was only a type; and by constant recourse to the Word of God, and by the repentance which that Word produces in us, we prove the efficacy of the death of Christ to maintain us in the position of acceptance and access to God, which redemption gives us. When a Christian whose secular pursuits are uncongenial to the spiritual life turns away from them to acts of worship or of service, he can appreciate the words of the exhortation, "Let us draw near . . . having our hearts sprinkled from an evil conscience."

But the exhortation adds, "and our bodies washed with pure water." Without the sprinkling of the water of purification, the bath would be unavailing; and to resort to the sprinkling while neglecting the bath would be to appeal to the atoning work of Christ without turning away from evil. For such is the figurative meaning of washing in Scripture. It signifies only and always *practical* purity. To read

[1] 1 Pet. i. 23.

baptism into the passage is to fritter away its force and meaning, for it relates to the privileges and responsibilities of the Christian life, and not to the position accorded to the sinner on his coming to Christ for salvation. And more than this, such a perversion of the text implies the confounding of Christian baptism with the pagan rite of the Eleusinian mysteries.[1]

---

[1] "The question before us is how the simple baptism of the New Testament, administered to those who professed belief in Christ, as an acknowledgment by them of submission to His Lordship over them and their identification with Him in death, was supplanted in the cult of 'the historic Church' by a mystic rite by which the sinner is cleansed from sin and, as Augustine has it, 'born of the bowels of the Church.' Here is the solution of the problem. This brief notice of the Eleusinian mysteries has been given almost entirely in borrowed words (Prof. Sir W. Ramsay), lest any should suppose the facts are misstated for a purpose. And in the sequel, for the same reason, the language of another shall be followed still more closely."

The reference here is to the *Hibbert Lectures*, 1888, by Dr. Hatch of Oxford. That great book gives overwhelming proof that the baptism of "the historic Church" is purely pagan, derived from the Eleusinian mysteries, not merely as regards its main characteristics as a laver of regeneration and soul-cleansing, but as to all its details and even its terminology. The present author's book from which the above sentences are quoted, contains lengthy extracts from Hatch, and discusses the whole question (*The Buddha of Christendom*—reissued in 1908 under the title of *The Bible or the Church*).

6

ASPECTS OF HIS WORK

IN a certain house there hangs a notable picture
which commemorates a great historic event,
and contains portraits of all the notable per-
sonages who took part in it. A sketch-plan,
which had been prepared in advance, indicated
the name and rank of each of them; but when
the picture itself was hung upon the wall, there
seemed to be no further need of the sketch, and
so it was thrown away. And to-day if you
ask for particulars about the various portraits,
most members of the circle will tell you that
such details have no interest for them : it is
the central figure alone that they think about,
and it is the picture as a whole that they value.
Or if any of the house-party should make a
more sympathetic response to your inquiries,
you will get conflicting answers from them,
for they are all at sea upon the subject.

This parable, suggested by the study of
Hebrews, may serve to illustrate our efforts
to understand the evangelical teaching of the
New Testament, if the key-plan of Old Testament typology be neglected. For, though the

sacrificial work of Christ has as many aspects
as there are great typical sacrifices in the Pentateuch, the Passover and the Sin-offering hold a
practically exclusive prominence in our theology.
And yet the Passover, though in a sense the
basis of all the rest, has no place in Hebrews;[1]
and the Sin-offering holds a subordinate position
in the doctrinal teaching of the Epistle.

The ninth chapter will help to guide us
aright in the use of these many types. As
they all point to Christ, we may lose important
truth if we neglect any one of them. But
we must not suppose that His *sacrificial* work
was marked by successive stages.[2] And yet
we need to distinguish between these types.
An uninstructed reader, for example, would
probably fail to notice that verses 12 and 13
point to three entirely different offerings. For
verse 12 (compare verse 19) refers to the Covenant sacrifice of Exodus xxiv.; and verse 13
to the two great sin-offerings of Leviticus xvi.
and Numbers xix.

And though, perhaps, the uninstructed reader

---

[1] See p. 21, *ante*.

[2] It is noteworthy that in this section of Hebrews (ix. and x.) the
Lord's Advent in all that it signified and all that it accomplished,
from His " coming into the world " to His return to His heavenly throne,
is spoken of as *one*. If such statements, *ex. gr.*, as x. 5; ix. 11; ix. 24,
&c., were prophecy, a reader might suppose that their fulfilment would
be a matter of days—if not of hours, like the ritual of the Day of
Atonement.

may fail to appreciate distinctions of this kind, he will eagerly seize upon another distinction which no pupil in the divine kindergarten of Bible typology can miss, namely, that while the types specified in Hebrews represent only what the death of Christ is to His people, yet in a most important aspect of it that death was for a lost world. And it is owing to ignorance of the typology, and of the distinctions which it teaches, that seemingly conflicting statements of Scripture have driven theologians into separate, if not hostile, camps, and have led ordinary Christians (like the owners of the picture in my parable) to ignore details altogether, and to rest content with general impressions.

When, for example, we read in one Scripture that Christ " gave Himself a ransom for all," and in another that He was " offered to bear the sins of many," we must not set ourselves to prove that " all " means only *some*, or that " many " is equivalent to *all;* but, knowing that no book in the world is so precise in its terminology as the New Testament, we shall turn to the key-picture of the Pentateuch, to find that here, as always, Scripture is perfectly accurate and consistent with itself.

Take, for example, two passages in the First Epistle of Peter, which are akin to the passages above quoted. In chapter i. 18, 19, we read,

" Ye were not redeemed with corruptible things
. . . but with the precious Blood of Christ,
as of a lamb without blemish and without
spot "; and in chapter ii. 24, " Who His own self
bare our sins in His own body to the tree." The
references here are unmistakable—in the one
case to the Paschal Lamb of Exodus xii.; in the
other, to the scapegoat of Leviticus xvi. But the
Passover was the sacrifice by which an enslaved
and doomed people obtained redemption, whereas,
in common with the other sacrifices of the law,
the sin-offering was for those who had been thus
redeemed.

To object that the Israelites were the " Covenant people " involves an anachronism, for the
covenant had not yet been inaugurated. And
to say that none but the Israelites could have
gained the shelter of the blood is wholly un-
warranted; for if, even after the covenant was
dedicated, such an outcast as " Rahab the harlot "
could come within the pale, we may be certain
that any Egyptian might have thrown in his
lot with Israel, and sought the shelter of the
blood. This suggestion is entirely in the spirit
of the law which permitted the stranger to eat
the Passover.[1]

In the case of the sin-offering, before the
victim was slain the offerer identified himself

[1] Num. ix. 14; and see Deut. xxiii. 7.

with it by placing his hands upon its head. But there was no such identification of the Israelite with the Paschal lamb. Its blood was shed and sprinkled upon the house, and all who sought the shelter of the blood escaped the death sentence pronounced upon Egypt. But, in contrast with this, on the Day of Atonement the sins of the redeemed people were laid upon the scapegoat,[1] and the victim bore them away to the wilderness—the desert aptly typifying "that undiscovered country from whose bourne no traveller returns." And so, in the language of the types, the inspired Apostle tells us that Christ " bare our sins to the tree." [2] *Our* sins— the sins of us who have been redeemed by the blood of the Paschal lamb.

For " bearing sins " is a figurative expression, and the figure is neither poetic nor yet forensic, but sacrificial ; and it comes from the great Day of Atonement. Therefore is it that in Scripture the Gospel for the unsaved is never stated in the language of the sin-offering. And a student of

---

[1] Lev. xvi. 21, 22.

[2] " Most modern scholars are agreed to reject ' *on* the tree ' in favour of the marginal ' to.' " Dean Alford's gloss here is, " took them to the tree, and offered them up on it as an altar." Fancy offering up sins to God upon an altar! If we neglect the types—the language in which Christian truth is taught in the New Testament—no vagary of exegesis is too wild ! The imputation of the sinner's sin to Christ was the act of *God* (Isa. liii. 6.) " This is your hour and the power of darkness," the Lord exclaimed in Gethsemane : may not that hour have been the crisis ? Again and again the Lord spoke of it ; and till then no hand was ever laid on Him save in loving service.

the types will notice any violation of this rule as instinctively as a trained ear will detect a discord. Or if he should find any seeming exceptions, he will rightly attribute them to the wording of our English versions.

The utterance of the Baptist, recorded in John i. 29, is a case in point. "Behold the Lamb of God, which taketh away the sin of the world." This is not translation merely, it savours of exegesis. "Who beareth the sin of the world" is what the Baptist said. His words were not a prophecy of what Christ would accomplish by His death, but a statement of what He was in His life. Mark the present tense, "Who *is bearing*." And while the word used in 1 Peter ii. 24, and in kindred passages, is a sacrificial term, we have here an ordinary word for lifting and carrying burdens. When the Lord sighed in healing the deaf mute by the Sea of Galilee, [1] and when He groaned and wept at the grave of Lazarus, He took upon Himself, as it were, the infirmities and sorrows which He relieved, and made them His own. And in this pregnant sense it was that He bore the world's sin. In this sense of the word He was manifested to bear sins, [2] and in no other sense was He a sin-bearer during His earthly life.

---

[1] Mark vii. 34.

[2] 1 John iii. 5, R.V. (margin). The word is αἴρω, as in John i. 29. See its use in John v. 8, 9, 10, 11, 12, *ex. gr.*

The imputation of sin to Christ was entirely the act of God. And the twenty-second Psalm tells of His anguish when He reached that crisis of His mission, and passing under the awful cloud " became a curse for us." But to suppose that the twenty-second Psalm expresses His relations with the Father during the years of His ministry gives proof that in the religious sphere there is nothing too profane, and nothing too false, to be believed. He was " manifested" to bear human sins and sorrows, for the facts of His life and death on earth are matters of evidence, and none but fools deny them. But that He was the Son of God, and that He " died for our sins according to the Scriptures " —this is altogether matter of revelation, and none but fools would believe it on mere human testimony.

There is no element of deception or of artifice in the Gospel. The Lord commissioned His Apostles to proclaim forgiveness of sins among all nations.[1] And from one of the sermons recorded in Acts we know in what sense they understood His words. " Through Him is preached unto you forgiveness of sins," said Paul at Pisidian Antioch.[2] And this because (as he declared at Corinth—the message being given him by express revelation) " Christ died

---

[1] Luke xxiv. 47.   [2] Acts xiii. 38.

for our sins, according to the Scriptures." [1] The truth of this is in no respect modified by the further truth that when the believing sinner receives Christ, he becomes identified with Him in the sin-offering sense. For the passover was as true as the sin-offering. And the Antioch sermon discloses a kindred advance in truth; for, to the proclamation of the amnesty, the Apostle added, "And all who believe are justified."

"Justified freely by His grace," as we read in Romans iii. 24. The Jew indeed had "the promises made unto the Fathers," but we Gentiles (being "strangers from the covenants of promise") "glorify God for His *mercy*." [2] We owe everything to grace; and to speak of grace for a favoured few, if it do not imply a contradiction in terms, is at least an utterly inadequate statement of truth. "For the grace of God has appeared, salvation-bringing *to all men*." [3] And God is "willing that *all men* should be saved." [4] Language could not be more explicit and unequivocal; and to question whether these statements are true and to be taken "at their face value," is profanely to charge the Word of God with deception of a kind that would not be tolerated as between man and man. [5]

---

[1] 1 Cor. xv. 3.   [2] Rom. xv. 8, 9.   [3] Tit. ii. 11.   [4] 1 Tim. ii. 4.
[5] The writer is not unaware of what is said to the contrary. He has dealt with the subject fully in his book, *The Gospel and its Ministry*. Published by Kregel Publications , 1978.

In the parable of the Great Supper,[1] the Lord likens us Gentile Christians to the tramps and waifs of the highways and the city streets, who in Divine mercy have been gathered to the feast which the privileged people spurned. And yet when we come within, we find a place prepared and reserved for each of us, as though we were specially invited guests. But the effect produced on some people by this amazing mystery of grace is that they return to the streets and highways, not to obey the Master's orders to publish the good news to "the poor and the maimed and the halt and the blind," but to announce that the places are limited, and that it is all settled who shall occupy them.

The mention of the covenants in this section of Hebrews throws light upon this subject, and moreover it has a special interest for the Bible student. The Old Testament quotations in chapter viii. relate to the "new covenant with the house of Israel and with the house of Judah," a covenant which will bring "the times of refreshing" that fill so large a place in Hebrew prophecy.[2] And they are quoted, not to establish the fact of a new covenant—for that no Israelite would question—but because the fact gives proof that the Mosaic covenant

---

[1] Luke xiv. 16–24.　　　　[2] See p. 87, *post.*

is superseded. But Scripture knows nothing of a covenant with Gentiles, and the question arises, where do we come in? The Greek word *diathēkē* signifies both "covenant" and "testament"; and while to the covenant there are two parties and a "mediator," a testament depends only on the will of the testator, and it becomes operative at his death. And so, up to the fifteenth verse of Hebrews ix., the word is used in the Old Testament sense, but in the sixteenth verse it assumes the alternative meaning of "testament."[1] Our spiritual and eternal blessings do not depend on a covenant made with us, but upon a testament under which we are beneficiaries.

And if we have learned to mark the accuracy of Holy Scripture, we shall not fail to notice how the difference between the relations of Hebrews and of Gentiles to the new covenant is recognised in the institution of the Lord's Supper. For the favoured people had access to the blood in virtue of the covenant, whereas we Gentiles come within the covenant in virtue of the blood. In the "Hebrew" Gospel, there-

---

[1] "The writer to the Hebrews in ix. 16 *sqq.* substitutes for the meaning *covenant*, which *diathēkē* bears elsewhere in the Epistle, that of *testament*, and likens Christ to the testator" (Grimm's *Lexicon*). Save only in two passages *diathēkē* is always the Septuagint rendering of the Hebrew word *berith*. This explains why the word has a double meaning in the New Testament; but in his *Light from the Ancient East* Prof. Deissmann shows that with all Greek-speaking peoples in the first century, the only meaning in common use was "testament."

fore, we read, " This is My blood of the new covenant " [1] whereas in the " Gentile " Gospel it is " This cup is the new covenant in My blood." [2]

While the old covenant had an earthly sanctuary and a human priesthood, the sanctuary of the new covenant is heaven itself, and the Great Priest who ministers there is no other than the Son of God. This, the Apostle declares, is " the chief point " of all he has said (chap. viii. 1, R.V.). And these great facts of the Christian revelation sweep away the whole structure of the false cult of Christendom. That cult would have us believe that every man upon whose head a bishop's consecrating hands have been placed is a sacrificing priest, with powers and privileges higher than those which pertained to the divinely appointed priests in Israel. But so exclusive are the prerogatives of the sons of Aaron, that while on earth not even the Lord Jesus Christ could share them. [3] What a staggering fact it is that, during His earthly ministry, the Son of God Himself could not pass within the veil which screened the antechamber to the holy shrine! And yet that place of worship was merely " a sanctuary of this world," and Jewish priests " went in continually."

---

[1] Matt. xxvi. 28. [2] Luke xxii. 20.
[3] Heb. viii. 4. See p. 26 f., *ante.*

The very existence of this antechamber—the "first tabernacle" of Hebrews—gave proof that "the way into the holiest of all was not yet made manifest." [1]   An earthly place of worship is proof that the heavenly place of worship is still closed. The Apostle therefore warned the Hebrew Christians that to set up such a place of worship, with an earthly priesthood, was apostasy, for it denied the efficacy of the work of Christ. And by this test the false religion of Christendom, with its earthly shrines and its earthly priesthood, is proved to be outside the pale of true Christianity. [2]

---

[1] See Bishop Lightfoot's words quoted on p. 77.   The mention of the contents of the ark of the covenant in chap. ix. 4, shows how definitely it is the Tabernacle and not the Temple on which the teaching of the Epistle is based.   See 1 Kings viii. 9.   And the difficulty created by the mention of the Golden Altar of incense admits of a solution that is at once simple and instructive.   The suggestion of certain foreign expositors, that the Apostle blundered on such a matter, savours of the ignorance and conceit of Gentile exegesis.   Though it stood in "the first tabernacle," and not within the veil, yet, as its use clearly indicated (Lev. xvi. 12, 13), and as 1 Kings vi. 22 (see R.V.) states in express terms, it "belonged to the oracle."   The significance of this is made clear by such passages as Exod. xxx. 6, 10, and xl. 5.

I am assuming, though not without some doubt, that in Heb. ix. 4, the R.V. is correct in reading "altar," and not "censer."   The Greek word bears either meaning.   And if A.V. be right, it is obvious that as Aaron was to enter the holiest in a cloud of incense, the censer, though it "belonged to the oracle," must have been kept outside the veil.

[2] Heb. ix. 8.

7

A GREAT PRIEST

" HAVING a Great Priest over the house of
God." [1] Upon this depends our right of access
to the divine presence. For His priesthood is
a necessity, not only because of human infirmity
and need, but because of the holiness and
majesty of God. And yet, owing to our in-
veterate habit of regarding redemption from
our own standpoint, we forget this highest
aspect of the truth.

In the miracles of Scripture within the sphere
of the natural, there is nothing so seemingly
incredible as that God should allow a sinner
to come into His presence. Yet such is the
blindness of unspiritual men, that they carp at
the miracles, while treating these amazing truths
of grace as commonplaces of Evangelical doctrine.
A comparison between our Christian hymn-
books and the old Hebrew Psalms will indicate
how much lower is our conception of God, than
that of the spiritual Israelite of a bygone age.

---

[1] Heb. x. 21, R.V.   There is probably a reference here to Zech. v.
11, where the Greek version reads, " Jesus (*i.e.* Joshua) the great
priest " ; of whom the thirteenth verse says, " he shall bear the glory,
and shall sit and rule upon his throne, and he shall be a priest
upon his throne."

And we forget that man is not the only created being in the universe. Of the Gospel of our salvation it is written, " which things angels desire to look into." No good man would refuse to meet a repentant criminal or magdalen. But none save a fanatic or a fool would bring such into his home, and give them a place of special nearness and honour in his family and household. And yet this would be but a paltry illustration of what the grace of God has done for sinful men. " While the first tabernacle was yet standing," not even the holiest of the sons of the old covenant, not even the divinely appointed priests, were allowed to enter His holy presence. But under the new covenant the worst of men may receive not only pardon and peace in Christ, but a right of access to God. And this would be impossible were it not for the presence of Christ at the right hand of the Majesty on high : it might well strain the allegiance of the heavenly host, and raise doubts respecting the righteousness and holiness of God. But all this is well-nigh forgotten, because of our unworthy appreciation of what is due to God, and our false estimate of what is due to man.

That the Son of God—He who was with God, and was God, the brightness of His glory and the express image of His person, He who upholds

all things by the word of His power—came down
to earth to take part of flesh and blood, and here
to live a life of poverty and suffering and reproach, " despised and rejected of men," and to
die a death of infamy as a common malefactor ;
and that now, with " all power in heaven and on
earth," He is at the right hand of God, to make
atonement and intercession for us, and to sympathise and succour in all the needs and trials of
our chequered life—if men were not so superstitious and stupid in the religious sphere, this
would divide the world into two hostile camps,
and every one would become either a devout
worshipper or an open infidel. For in all the
fables of the false religions of the world there is
nothing so utterly incredible as this.

But breaking away from this train of thought,
let us try to realise in some little measure what
His Priesthood means for those who are His own.
If we are saved from wrath by what He has
done for us, and what He is to us, our access to
the divine presence depends on what He is to
God for us. But we do well here to shun all
fanciful thoughts and phrases, and to keep closely
to what is revealed in Scripture. Phrases in
common use, as, for example, that He " pleads
His blood " before the throne, are greatly to
be deprecated. In coming into the world
to accomplish the work of redemption, He

was doing the will of God; and in His High-priestly work for us, He is doing the will of God in glory now. His present work of atonement and intercession are not needed to appease an alienated Diety, nor to overcome divine unwillingness to bless a sinner. But He thus makes it possible for God to bless us consistently with all that He is, and all that He has declared Himself to be. And this, moreover, is a public fact in heaven. For our redemption is no " back-stairs " business. Our " drawing near " to the divine presence is in open view of all the heavenly host;[1] and the " principalities and powers in heavenly places " will find in it a revelation of " the manifold wisdom of God."[2]

Had the Lord not taken part of flesh and blood, the death to which we owe our redemption would have been impossible. But though the sufferings of His sojourn upon earth may not have been essential to His redeeming work, it is to that life we owe it that as our High-priest He can be touched with the feeling of our infirmities. And this, moreover, even in respect of the common troubles and privations of the humblest lot.

Our pity is stirred at times by hearing of destitute and homeless paupers who spend their nights in the streets of our great cities. If a

---

[1] Such is the force of chap. xii. 22.   [2] Eph. iii. 10.

true and trusting child of God could be found in such a company—and I say "if" advisedly, for after a long and varied experience I would say with David, "I have not seen *the righteous* forsaken"—what peace might guard the heart of such an one in remembering that the Lord Himself knew what it meant to be hungry! And homeless, too; for we recall His words, "Foxes have holes, and the birds of the air have nests, but the Son of Man hath not where to lay His head." And in dark days of persecution, before the Reformation stamped out the fires of Smithfield, the martyrs could look away from earth to heaven, rejoicing in the remembrance that their Lord and Saviour "was made perfect through suffering," and "endured such contradiction of sinners against Himself."

But the trials which engross the thoughts of most of us are of a baser kind. Can we look for divine sympathy as we resist temptations due to evil lusts and passions? The Scripture is definite that He "was *in all points* tempted like as we are." But the Commentaries tell us that the added words, "yet without sin," do not mean that He never fell, but that "in all His temptations, whether as to their origin, their process, or their results, sin had nothing in Him." And this seems to separate Him from us by a barrier which is impassable.

But a right appreciation of the essential character of sin will break that barrier down, and teach us to "come boldly to the throne of grace, that we may obtain mercy and find grace to help in time of need."

"Sin is the transgression of the law." This perversion of the words of Scripture robs us of important truth. Law-breaking is merely one phase of sin. In its essence "Sin is lawlessness"[1]—the assertion of our own will against the will of God. And further, we construe the word "tempt" in its sinister and secondary acceptation as inciting to what is morally evil. It means first and chiefly to prove, or try, or test. And it is in this sense that the Greek term is used in the majority of its occurrences in the New Testament. In this sense alone it is that men are said to be tempted of God. And thus it was that Christ was "tempted." There is no sin in satisfying a natural craving for food when we are hungry, and when food is within our reach. And yet He bore the pangs of hunger, although by a touch He could make food for a multitude of starving men, and by a word He might have changed the stones to bread. But he was treading the path of absolute dependence upon His Father; and no pangs of hunger or of thirst, no sense

---

[1] ἡ ἁμαρτία ἐστὶν ἡ ἀνομία (1 John iii. 4).

of homelessness, could make Him swerve from that lonely and tragic path.

And if Christians ever give a thought to the sufferings of His life on earth, it is for the most part only in relation to such privations and needs as these. And yet not even the most exquisitely sensitive of mortals can realise what the sufferings of that life must have been to Him. The immorality, the baseness, the meanness, the very vulgarities of men, "the contradiction of sinners"—"every day they wrest my words"[1]—who can estimate what all this was to Him? What a long drawn-out martyrdom must that life have been!

And what may we dare to say about Gethsemane? When the Lord was "tempted of the Devil" He spurned the thought of reaching the glory save by the path which led to death. And the suggestion is impious that He faltered at the last. But Scripture warrants our believing that while the horrors and agonies of Calvary give proof of the limitlessness of divine love to man, they could add nothing to either the preciousness or the efficacy of the blood of our redemption. And may not this throw light upon the mystery of His prayer in the garden? Sure it is that the cup which, He pleaded, might pass from Him was not the death He had come to die. But

[1] Ps. lvi. 5.

might He not be spared the attendant horrors, as foretold in the Psalms, and detailed in the Gospel narratives?

One element in His sufferings, for example, which we pass almost unnoticed, may have been to Him more cruel even than physical pain. A pure and delicate woman can possibly appreciate in some measure what an ordeal it must have been to hang in nakedness upon the Cross, a public spectacle to that "great company of people, and of women," that had followed Him to Golgotha. "And sitting down they watched Him there," the Gospel narrative records: a cruelly literal fulfilment of His words by the Holy Spirit in the twenty-second Psalm, "They look and stare upon Me!" [1]

If, as He had said in Gethsemane, a prayer would have brought legions of angels to His help, we may be sure that He might have sought immunity from all these shameful indignities and cruelties. For His sufferings were not endured in obedience to an iron decree of fate, but in submission to His Father's will. Therefore it was—therefore, and not in the spirit of a stoic—that He drank that cup of suffering to the dregs. He might, as I venture reverently to suggest, have claimed relief. But

---

[1] And the position of these words in the Psalm would indicate that this was no mere incident in His sufferings, but a climax.

we recall His words in Gethsemane, " How then
shall the Scriptures be fulfilled !" and His words
after the resurrection, " Ought not Christ to
have suffered these things ?" and again, " That
all things must be fulfilled that were written
in the law of Moses, and in the prophets, and *in
the Psalms*, concerning Me."   And yet we doubt
and cavil at the word that He was in all things
tempted like as we are ! The trial surely was in
His case all the fiercer just because it was not
an incitement to sin in the sense of moral evil,
but merely to a turning aside from the path
of dependent obedience.

The doubt and the cavil are based upon the
fact that we are sinful and He was sinless; for
on this ground it is that we question whether
He can understand our struggles. This is as
unintelligent as it is dishonouring to Him. Is
it only the reclaimed drunkard who can help
one who is a slave to drink ? Can no woman
help a magdalen unless she herself has fallen ?
The struggles of pure and holy souls, though
waged in a different sphere, may be keener
far than any which coarser natures ever know.
And if this be true even on the plane of our
fallen humanity, it is far more true of Him.

If we yield to sin and have recourse to evil
practices, we need not look to Him for *sympathy*,
though a penitent confession will bring pardon

full and free through His atoning work. But
an incitement or tendency to evil if resisted
and kept down is reckoned an " infirmity," and
we can look with confidence to One who can
be " touched with the feeling of our infirmities "
—to One who in doing the will of God has
suffered as we have never suffered, as we, with
our fallen nature, are incapable of suffering.

Forgetting this we miss the significance of
the fourth verse of chapter xii., " Ye have not
yet resisted unto blood." It is still the imagery
of the arena ; but instead of the race, as in the
opening verses of the chapter, it is now the
combat. That brutal " prize-fight " which lately
agitated all America was preceded by a series
of " sparring matches " between noted pugilists.
Our " striving against sin " is compared with
combats such as theirs, in which no blood was
drawn. Hence the exhortation which immediately precedes the above-quoted words : " Consider Him that endured such contradiction of
sinners against Himself, lest ye be wearied and
faint in your minds." Every day of His earthly
life two paths lay open to His choice. The
one the path of suffering in doing His Father's
will ; the other a path of peace and ease, yet
just as free from every element of what *we*
call sin. And every day He made choice of
the martyr path ; for Gethsemane was but an

intenser and more terrible phase of the struggle of His daily life. Yes, yes! "He was in all points tried as we are, without sin." And He who never faltered and never failed "is able to save to the uttermost them that come unto God by Him, seeing He ever liveth to make intercession for them."

8

WHY THE TABERNACLE?

THE interesting question has been often raised, Why is it of the wilderness Tabernacle, and not of the Jerusalem Temple, that the Epistle to the Hebrews speaks? The historical narrative of King David's reign clearly suggests that the Tabernacle represented the divine purpose, and that the Temple was a concession to David's desire and prayer.[1] For God never refuses a "burnt-offering" from the humble and true-hearted. But as God did accept that offering, the question remains, why the Temple has no place in Hebrews. And perhaps one reason may be in order thus to exclude the element of merely superstitious awe which a splendid shrine is fitted to excite. The divine presence alone can constitute "a place of worship" in the deeper, truer sense; and the exhortation to "draw near" raises the question, what and where is "the holy place" which we are bidden to approach? And to this all-important question the ninth chapter supplies the answer.

---

[1] 2 Sam. vii.; 1 Chron. xvii.

The veil which was rent when the Saviour died was not the curtain through which "the priests went always into the first tabernacle," but the inner veil which no one but the high priest might pass, and that only on the Day of Atonement. That veil bore testimony to the presence of God, and also to the sinner's unfitness to approach Him. And the rending of it had also a twofold significance. It indicated the fulfilment of the solemn words with which the Lord had turned away from the holy city, "Behold your house is left unto you desolate"; and it symbolised that the true worshipper, being purged from his sin by the sacrifice of Calvary, might enter the divine presence. But though the way is open, who will dare to approach? The twenty-second verse of the tenth chapter, which we have been considering, deals only with the worshipper viewed as here on earth, and far more is needed if we are to draw nigh to God.

From the Epistle to the Romans we learn how a sinner can stand before a righteous God, but the Epistle to the Hebrews teaches the far deeper and more amazing truth that he may approach a God of infinite holiness. Nor is this all, for the exhortation reads, "Having *boldness* to enter into the holy place . . . let us draw near." How can this be possible?

In these days we are accustomed to hear that the solemnities of the Jewish cult belonged to the ignorant childhood of the human race, and that this enlightened age has a worthier estimate of the dignity of man. But such thoughts as these, instead of betokening greater moral enlightenment, give proof of spiritual darkness and death. Those who by faith have learned the meaning of the Cross of Christ can form a far higher estimate of the holiness of God than could the saintliest of saints in a bygone age. In that age His people had to do with a mount that might be touched and that burned with fire, and with blackness and darkness and tempest, and the awful voice which filled their hearts with terror;[1] whereas we in these "last days" are come to eternal realities more awful still, of which those sights and sounds were merely symbols. And to us it is that the exhortation is addressed, "Let us have grace whereby we may serve God acceptably, with reverence and godly fear; for our God is a consuming fire." The secret of our boldness is not to be found in a false estimate of the dignity of man, and still less does it depend on ignoring what is due to the majesty of God. Our confidence is based on knowing our glorious Saviour, and the eternal

---

[1] Chap. xii. 18, 19.

redemption He has brought us. The confidence
of faith has nothing in common with presumption begotten of ignorance and error.

What then are the facts and truths on which
our faith intelligently rests? What is the significance of these figurative words—the veil,
the blood? As already noticed, the veil had
a twofold aspect. It barred the entrance to
the holy place, and yet it was the way by
which the high-priest passed in. What meaning then shall we give to the words "the veil,
that is to say, *His flesh*"? The word "flesh"
sometimes symbolises our evil nature, but it
is never so used in Hebrews. In this Epistle
it always signifies the "natural body."[1] The
rent veil then is the broken body of Christ.
It is by "a new and living way" that we
approach, but it is in virtue of His death that
that way is open to us.

But if the rent veil symbolises the death
of Christ, is the mention of the blood a mere
repetition? By no means. It is upon the
death of Christ, regarded as a great objective
fact, that our redemption rests, whereas *the
blood* always speaks to us of His death in
relation to its effects or its application to ourselves. How then are we to understand the

---

[1] The word occurs in chap. ii. 14; v. 7; ix. 10 (carnal); ix. 13;
x. 20; and xii. 9.

words, "Having boldness to enter into the holy place in (virtue of) the blood of Jesus"? How would the Hebrew Christian have interpreted them? Not, we may be sure, by that strange vagary of exegesis, that it was as forerunner of His people raised to an equality with Himself in His High-priestly rank, that Christ entered the heavenlies with His own blood, and that we enter, as His fellow-priests, by the same blood.

It is noteworthy that the only book of the New Testament which tells of the High-priesthood of Christ never once refers explicitly to the priesthood of His people; for it is *as worshippers* that we are bidden to draw near. No less noteworthy is it that, as we have seen, Aaron laid aside his high-priestly garments before he passed within the veil with the blood of the sin-offering, thus indicating (for such is the exquisite accuracy of the types of Scripture) that his act, though typical of the work of Christ, was not typical of His High-priestly work. For it was not as High-priest that Christ entered the heavenlies "by His own blood." Aaron's entering in was a continually repeated ordinance, and this because the typical sin-offerings could not "take away sins"; but Christ's entering in was a never-to-be-repeated act. And then it was that, having for ever put away sin by the sacrifice of Himself, He was "called" of God High-priest after the order of Melchisedek.[1]

Can we doubt then that the Hebrew Christians, reading the verse in the light of the types, and marking, as they would, the significance of the words here employed, in contrast with those used of Christ's entering the heavenlies,[2] would read the exhortation thus: "Having therefore, brethren, boldness in virtue of the blood of Jesus to enter into the holy place . . . let us draw near"? Our confidence depends on what the death of Christ is to us, and what it is to God on our behalf. And this we learn from the preceding verses. Verse 14 declares that "by one offering He hath perfected for ever the sanctified ones." And the seventeenth verse adds, "And their sins and iniquities will I remember no more." Worshippers perfected, and sins forgotten—this is what the blood has gained for us. What ground there is here for "boldness"! And yet even this is not enough. Not even all this wonderful provision would be sufficient: hence the added words, "And having a Great Priest over the house of God." For the sanctuary is heaven itself, where the glorious beings whose

---

[1] See p. 26, *ante*. [2] In ix. 12 it is διά; here in x. 19 it is ἐν.

home is there fall upon their faces as they worship.[1]

The Jew understood, though we Gentiles miss it, the difference between a sanctuary and a synagogue. In the loose sense in which we use that phrase, every synagogue was " a place of worship," but in fact the only sanctuary was the holy Temple. And when, in speaking of the time when men should no longer worship in Jerusalem, the Lord declared that " the true worshippers shall worship the Father in spirit and in truth," He did not mean to teach that synagogues would become sanctuaries, but that spiritual worshippers, having access to the true and heavenly sanctuary, would no longer need " a sanctuary of this world." " I have many things to say, but ye cannot bear them now," explains the gap in His teaching here. That Jerusalem was no longer to be the place of worship must have seemed indeed " a hard saying " to His hearers. But not until the Spirit of truth had come to lead His people into all truth, could they bear the revelation that heaven itself was to be the place of worship for those whom the Father sought to worship Him. Till then, the words would have had no meaning for His disciples.

With the great majority of Christians, they

---

[1] Rev. vii. 11 ; xi. 16.

have no meaning still. But "true worshippers" understand them; and whether they bow in a stately cathedral, or "by a river-side where prayer is wont to be made," they know what it means to "worship the Father in spirit and in truth." But the religion of Christendom, with its sham priests and its "sanctuaries of this world," denies the work of Christ, and is utterly antichristian. For, as Bishop Lightfoot of Durham writes, "It (the kingdom of Christ) has no sacred days or seasons, no special sanctuaries, because every time and every place alike are holy. Above all it has no sacerdotal system. It interposes no sacrificial tribe or class between God and man. . . . For conducting religious worship it became necessary to appoint special officers. But the priestly functions and privileges of the Christian people are never regarded as transferred or even delegated to these officers . . . the sacerdotal title is never once conferred upon them. The only priests under the Gospel, designated as such in the New Testament, are the saints, the members of the Christian brotherhood. As individuals all Christians are priests alike." [1]

Such is the security of the Christian's position; such the solemnity and dignity of Christian worship. How natural the added exhortation,

---

[1] *Philippians,* p. 181.

" Let us hold fast the confession of our hope."
And the note that vibrates through it all is
this word " boldness." [1] But as " all people of
discernment " know, in religion everything is
unreal, and words are never to be taken at
their face value! So the chapter turns aside
at once to warn us that boldness is not for
such as we are, and that our confession should
be pitched in a minor key! I appeal to the
reader whether this is not the meaning usually
put upon the passage. But what is the Apostle's
own statement of its purpose? The thirty-fifth
verse gives the answer: " Therefore cast not
away your boldness which hath great recompense
of reward." The very words which are used
to undermine faith are intended as a warning
against allowing faith to falter.

The wilful sin here warned against was turning back to Judaism, that religion which Christ
by His coming had fulfilled. It was to set up
again " the first tabernacle "—the place of service
of sacrificing priests, and thus to deny that
the way into the holiest was open. And this
was to tread under foot the Son of God, to
treat His blood as common—no better than
that of calves and goats, and to do despite
to the Spirit of grace. As Dean Alford puts
it, " It is the sin of apostasy from Christ back

---

[1] The word *parrēsia* occurs in chap. iii. 6 ; iv. 16 ; x. 19 and 35.

to the state which preceded the reception of Christ, viz. Judaism." [1]

And this could have but one ending—divine vengeance: "It is a fearful thing to fall into the hands of the living God" (verses 30, 31). But while thus warning them of the issue of that false path, he had no fear of their pursuing it (verses 32–34). And so, in still more explicit words, he again reminds them of the Christian hope (verses 35–37). These words recall the parenthesis of chapters iii. and iv. about the Sabbath-rest, and they may conveniently be considered in connection with it.

---

[1] Dean Alford adds, "This is the ground-sin of all other sins. Notice the present, not the aor. past. 'If we be found wilfully sinning,' not 'if we have wilfully sinned,' at that Day. It is not of an act, or of any number of acts of sin, that the writer is speaking, which might be repented of and blotted out."

Similar to this is the warning of the sixth chapter. Their turning back to Judaism gave proof that they were ignorant of the very rudiments, "the first principles of Christ," which Judaism taught (chap. v. 12 ; vi. 1). But instead of sending them back to that school, he warns them that thus they would "be crucifying to themselves the Son of God afresh"—mark the present tense again ; and for such apostasy there was no remedy. Not that he really believed they would sin thus (verses 9–12). But in Scripture a path is judged by the goal to which it leads.

9

THE RETURN OF CHRIST

"There remaineth a Sabbath-rest for the people of God." The Commentaries fail us here. Information about the works of a watch, however interesting it may be, does not seem opportune when we want to know the time. And our desire to know about that Sabbath-rest cannot be satisfied by learned criticisms of the Apostle's quotations from the Old Testament.

We may say at once that if that section of the Epistle means merely that a justified sinner can have peace with God, we can afford to ignore it altogether, for this truth is still more plainly taught in a single verse in Romans. But we must not treat Holy Scripture thus. And without attempting to solve all the difficulties which beset the passage, we may find perhaps that it throws not a little light upon a truth of the highest interest and importance to the Christian. The Apostle shows that the Sabbath-rest here spoken of was not the rest of creation, for the promise was given in the days of Moses. Neither was it the rest of

Canaan, for the promise was repeated " in
David." And that it was not realised in the
days of the kingdom is no less certain. But
no divine promise is ever cancelled, or can ever
fail; and therefore "there remaineth a Sabbath-
rest for the people of God, and some must
enter therein."

It is a popular error to suppose that the
forty years of Israel's wilderness wanderings
were a part of the divine purpose. When
God brought His people out of Egypt He
led them to Sinai; and there He gave them
His judgments and laws, and the ordinances of
the divine religion. But within two years from
the Exodus they were encamped at Kadesh-
Barnea, and from " the Mountain of the Amor-
ites " the promised land lay open before them,
and God bade them enter and take possession
of it. " But they could not enter in because
of unbelief." For the stern facts reported by
the spies whom they had sent into the land
were more real to them than the divine promises; and they rebelled against the command
of God, and threatened to stone their leaders.
For forty days the spies had "searched the
land"; and, in judgment on their sin, God declared that for forty years they should wander
in the wilderness; and that, save only Caleb
and Joshua, not a man of all the armed host

that marched out of Egypt on the Paschal night should ever enter Canaan.[1]

And when at last a new generation of Israelites entered the promised land, it was not by way of a triumphal march, such as that to which their fathers had been summoned, but through a death baptism in Jordan. What concerns us here, however, is the fact that the Sabbath-rest thus preached and thus forfeited was a *corporate*, and not a personal, blessing.

Has all this no voice for us? In the Apostolic age the people of God were taught to look for a Sabbath-rest, through the return of Christ. And in these days of flippant unbelief, when that hope is declared to have been a delusion or a blunder, we do well to recall the Apostle Peter's words, " We have not followed cunningly devised fables, when we made known unto you the power and coming of our Lord Jesus Christ."[2]

But what has become of that hope? The passage of the Jordan was not the fulfilment of the promise forfeited by Israel's unfaithfulness eight-and-thirty years before. And death is not the fulfilment of the hope which, for half of eight-and-thirty centuries, the unfaithfulness of the Professing Church has barred. I speak advisedly, for, even before the close

---

[1] Num. xiv.   [2] 2 Pet. i. 16.

of the Apostolic age, that hope had been let slip. It is ignored in our Christian creeds, and almost ignored in our standard theology. And no one who has any knowledge of Church History will pretend that, at any epoch in the past, " the Christian Church" was in a condition to receive the fulfilment of it.

In proof of this statement I might " put in " (as the lawyers would say) a whole library of standard works. But two brief quotations must suffice.

" I know not " (says the author of the Bampton Lectures, 1864) "how any man, in closing the Epistles, could expect to find the subsequent history of the Church essentially different from what it is. In these writings we seem, as it were, not to witness some passing storms which clear the air, but to feel the whole atmosphere charged with the elements of future tempest and death. Every moment the forces of evil show themselves more plainly." [1]

And of the Church in after times Dean Alford uses the following pregnant words in his commentary on the concluding parable of Matthew xii. After noticing its application to the Jewish people, he proceeds :—

" Strikingly parallel with this runs the history of the Christian Church. Not long after the

---

[1] Canon Bernard's *Progress of Doctrine*, Lecture VIII.

Apostolic times, the golden calves of idolatry
were set up by the Church of Rome. What
the effect of the captivity was to the Jews, that
of the Reformation has been to Christendom.
The first evil spirit has been cast out. But by
the growth of hypocrisy, secularity, and ration-
alism, the house has become empty, swept,
and garnished: swept and garnished by the de-
cencies of civilisation and discoveries of secular
knowledge, but empty of living and earnest
faith. And he must read prophecy but ill,
who does not see under all these seeming im-
provements the preparation for the final development of the man of sin, the great re-
possession, when idolatry and the seven worse
spirits shall bring the outward frame of so-
called Christendom to a fearful end."

In the light of all this let us now turn back to
Hebrews x. The exhortation to draw near with
a true heart in full assurance of faith, is followed
by the further exhortation to "hold fast the
confession of our hope." And to this is added
the word of cheer, " Ye see the day approaching."
In Scripture, as in common speech, "day" is
generally used to symbolise a time of light and
gladness. And so (after the parenthesis already
noticed) the Apostle returns to the promise of
"the day," and adds, " For yet a little while and
the Coming One will come and will not tarry."

But here again the Commentaries fail us. For the only future advent known to our creeds or noticed in most of our standard theological works is Christ's final coming to judgment—the awful climax of the great and terrible day of the Lord—when, the reign of grace being past and the era of mercy over, the flood-gates of divine vengeance will be opened upon a guilty world.

And so we are told that "the expression, *the day*, or *that day*, is almost always in the New Testament used of the day of *judgment*." It would be nearer the truth to say that it is *never* so used, save where, as for example in 1 Thessalonians v. 4, the context plainly indicates the reference to the day of wrath. And in that very passage the Apostle adds, reverting immediately to the ordinary meaning of the word, " Ye are all sons of light and sons of the day." This Hebrews passage is the counterpart of Romans xiii. 11, 12, " Now is our salvation nearer than when we believed: the night is far spent, the day is at hand." [1] No one but a monster could regard the coming of the great day of wrath as *a hope*. But the coming of Christ is the true hope of the people of God in every age.[2]

---

[1] See Appendix III., p. 168, *post.*

[2] We should be on our guard against the common error of confounding "the day of Jehovah "—the great day of wrath—with " the day of Christ" (Phil. i. 6, 10; ii. 16); or the day of our Lord Jesus Christ (1 Cor. i. 8 ; v. 5 ; 2 Cor. i. 14). In 2 Thess. ii. 2 we should read " the day *of the Lord,*" as in R.V.

Froude, the historian, has well described the difference between the Church of the New Testament and the Church of the Fathers as a change from the religion of Christ to the Christian religion. And "the Christian religion" jettisoned the teaching of Scripture on this subject, save in relation to the great final advent in the far distant future. A pandemonium ended by a bonfire might epigrammatically describe the scheme of the divine government of the world as travestied by much of our theology. True it is that this earth, which has been the scene of the pandemonium, shall yet be given up to fire, but not till every word of prophecy has been fulfilled; for no word of God can ever fail. "We, according to His promise, look for new heavens and a new earth"; but that belongs to an eternity to come. It is *in time*, as measured upon human calendars, and here on this earth of ours, now blighted by human sin, that divine goodness and power shall yet be displayed in righteous rule.

Of the fulfilment of this hope "God hath spoken by all His holy prophets since the world began"; and "the mystery of God"[1] is that its fulfilment is delayed. And yet the mass of those who profess to believe the Scriptures treat it as a dream of visionaries; and not a

[1] Rev. x. 7; xi. 15–18.

few there are who scoff at it. Though they pray "Thy kingdom come, Thy will be done on earth," they cannot tolerate the thought that the Lord will fulfil the prayer that He Himself has given us.

Here are the Apostle Peter's words to the Jerusalem Jews who had crucified the Messiah: "Repent ye therefore, and turn again, that your sins may be blotted out, that so there may come seasons of refreshing from the presence of the Lord; and that He may send the Christ who hath been appointed for you even Jesus: whom the heaven must receive until the times of restoration of all things, whereof God spake by the mouth of His holy prophets which have been since the world began." [1] "Seasons of refreshing," "the times of restoration of all things," or in other words, the times when everything shall be put right on this earth of ours, have a large place in all Hebrew prophecy from Moses to Malachi. And the Apostle proclaimed that a national repentance would bring them these times of gladness and blessing, by the return of the Messiah. But to "the Christian Church" to-day his divinely inspired words have no meaning. They are generally dismissed, indeed, as though they were merely the ravings of an enthusiast.

[1] Acts iii. 19–21, R.V.

The nation having proved impenitent, God deferred the realisation of these promises. Like their fathers in the days of Moses and of David, "they entered not in because of unbelief." The " Apostle to the Gentiles " received the call to his great ministry; and instead of " sending the Christ appointed for them," God sent them the awful judgment of the destruction of Jerusalem. The present dispensation, as we have seen, is episodical; and to " the Apostle to the Gentiles " the revelation was given that it will be brought to a close by a coming of Christ entirely unnoticed in Hebrew prophecy. [1] And if that coming is still delayed, the delay gives proof, not that the Word of God has failed, but that His people in this dispensation have followed in the evil ways of Israel of old. The Lord is called " the Coming One," and He will yet fulfil the promise of His Name. " Surely I am coming quickly " are His last recorded words, spoken from the throne in heaven. But their fulfilment awaits the response He looks for from His people, " Amen, come, Lord Jesus." [2]

---

[1] The Hebrew prophets speak of a time of widespread blessing to Gentiles. But the suggestion of a " Gentile dispensation " is unknown to Scripture until we reach the Epistle to the Romans, or possibly the Acts when read in the light of that Epistle. It is therefore a matter of course that the special hope of the people of God in this present age has no place in the Old Testament. See Appendix III.

[2] Rev. xxii. 20, 21.

There is not a Church in Christendom that would *corporately* pray that prayer to-day. For, as Bengel so truly says, "The Christian Churches have forgotten the hope of the Church." But though we cannot look with any confidence to organised Christianity, we may find encouragement in the records of God's dealings with His people in the past. At the first coming of Christ they who were "waiting for the redemption" were but a little company. It was a time of apostasy, as foretold in the last sad wail of Hebrew prophecy. But there mingled with that wail the gladdening words, "Then they that feared the Lord spake often one to another; and the Lord hearkened and heard, and a book of remembrance was written before Him for them that feared the Lord, and that thought upon His name."[1] And with these words before us may we not cherish the hope that in "the deepening gloom" which prevails in Christendom to-day,[2] those who think upon His Name

---

[1] Mal. iii. 16.

[2] The triumphs of the Gospel in various parts of heathendom to-day make the condition of Christendom seem all the more dark. Roman Catholic countries are rapidly lapsing to infidelity; and the change which has come over the religious condition of Great Britain in recent years is appalling. The National Church used to be Protestant; and organised Nonconformity was a great spiritual power. But now! And the prevailing evil is not spiritual death—for that there is a remedy, but the apostasy warned against in the Epistle to Laodicea (Rev. iii. 17).

may be led ere long with one heart to plead
that parting promise, and to unite in that
answering prayer?

To this end it is important to elucidate the
teaching of Scripture on the subject. Prevailing error crystallises round the expression
"The Second Advent," which, with most Christians, means the great day of wrath. The
phrase has no Scriptural sanction. It may
seem, perhaps, to find a warrant in the last
clause of Hebrews ix., but only at the cost
of misreading the passage, and separating it
from the context. For just as the geologist
sometimes comes upon a fragment of rock
that is foreign to its environment, so this
passage is deemed to be a prophetic fragment
embedded in a doctrinal exposition of Old
Testament typology. But it is, in fact, an
important step in the exposition which begins
with chapter ix., and ends with the twenty-
fifth verse of chapter x.

It has definite reference to the twenty-fourth
verse of the ninth chapter. When, on the Day of
Atonement, Aaron passed within the veil with
the blood of the sin-offering, the people waited
and watched till he came forth to bless them.
And his appearing again was the pledge and
proof that the sacrifice was accepted. So also,
we read, Christ was once offered to bear the

sins of many;[1] and to His waiting people He
will appear a second time, as did the high-priest
in Israel, "without sin unto salvation." That
this will have a literal fulfilment for the
earthly people we need not doubt; but it is
a great doctrinal truth for the people of God
in every age.

"The sufferings of Christ and the glories
that should follow"—such was the burden of
Messianic Hebrew prophecy. But how could
the difficulties be explained which underlay
such seemingly incompatible predictions? A
popular solution with many a Jew was the
figment of two Messiahs, one to suffer and the
other to reign. And the theology of Christendom, unwarned by this Jewish blunder, assumes
that all outstanding prophecy shall be fulfilled
by one great "Second Advent." And the many
Scriptures which cannot be made to fit in with
this theory are either discounted as mere hyper-
bole or poetry, or else they are dismissed as
the blundering of Apostles and Evangelists!

But even at the cost of forfeiting the respect
of "all people of discernment," we accept the
clear testimony of Holy Scripture. We must

---

[1] It is "the sins of *many*." Mark here the accuracy of Scripture.
For the reference is to the sin-offering of the Day of Atonement;
and it was the sins *of the people* that were put upon the victim (Lev.
xvi. 21). This element did not obtain in the great redemption sacrifice
of Exod. xii.

not presume to map out the future in detail, but we cannot fail to recognise that, beyond the present episodical dispensation, there lies a long vista of prophecy yet to be fulfilled on earth. For every promise of blessing both to Israel and to the world will yet be fulfilled as definitely as were the Scriptures relating to the sufferings of Christ.

No part of the prophecy of the Sacred Calendar shall fail. The present age is only the first of the great festivals that foretold in type the harvest of redemption. The sheaf of the first-fruits, primarily fulfilled in Christ, has a secondary and mystical fulfilment in " the Church which is His Body." But after Passover came Pentecost with its " two wave loaves " —Israel and Judah restored, and again in acceptance with God. And beyond the feast of Pentecost there still lie the principal harvest months, ending with the feast of Tabernacles— the great harvest-home of redemption, when an innumerable multitude of all nations and kindreds and peoples and tongues shall raise from earth such a redemption song as will lead the very angels of heaven to fall upon their faces before the throne in adoring worship.[1]

---

[1] Rev. vii. 9–12.

10

THE PATRIARCHS

In every age men of God have been men of faith. This is the theme of the eleventh chapter of Hebrews, that glorious "Westminster Abbey" of the Patriarchs. And to faith the future and the unseen become present realities. Reason testifies to the existence of God, and therefore none but fools are atheists.[1] And our natural and instinctive belief in God prepares us for a revelation; for it is unthinkable that a God whose creatures we are would leave us without light and guidance.

Faith may assume the phase of trust, and then it is near of kin to hope. But in its primary and simplest aspect, it declares itself by accepting the divine word, as a guileless child receives what falls from a parent's lips. And accordingly, as the first example of faith, the chapter refers to the earliest page of Scripture, which testifies both to the fact, and to the method, of creation. "Through faith we under-

---

[1] Ps. xiv. 1.

stand that the worlds [1] were framed by the word of God." [2]

The same principle explains how Abel offered an acceptable sacrifice. It was not that, being shrewder or more spiritual than Cain, he guessed aright what God required; but that he believed the primeval revelation which, pointing to the Great Sacrifice to come, ordained blood-shedding as the mode of approach to God. Of the fact of that revelation, the universality of sacrifice is overwhelming proof. For outside a lunatic asylum no human brain could ever have evolved the theory that killing an ox or a sheep would appease either God or man!

Abel believed God. But how are we to account for Enoch's faith? *By faith* he was translated that he should not see death. The only conceivable explanation of this is that he had a special promise. He, too, believed God.

And Noah's case is clearer still. He received a divine warning, and, believing God, "prepared an ark to the saving of his house." What signal proof is here that man is alienated from God, for Noah alone believed that warning.

---

[1] Both here and in chapter i. 2 the unlearned need to be warned that the R.V. marginal note is misleading. "Ages" is an *English* word, not Greek. In these passages, as occasionally in Alexandrian and Rabbinical Greek, the word which is usually translated "ages" means the material universe.

[2] Here it is not the *logos* but the *rēma*—the "God said" of Gen. i.

And through unbelief it was that "the world
that then was, perished," for the warning was
clear, and God gave time for repentance.
Distrust of God was the cause of the creature's
fall; most fitting it is, therefore, that faith
in God should be the turning-point of his
repentance.

As for Abraham, rightly is he called "the
father of all them that believe." Divine truth
can never clash with *reason*, but it may be
entirely opposed to experience, and seemingly
even to fact. So it was in his case. In regard
to the promise of a son, he had nothing to rest
upon but the bare word of God, unconfirmed
by anything to which he could appeal. The
Revisers' reading of Romans iv. 19 presents this
with the greatest definiteness: "He considered
his own body, now as good as dead, and the
deadness of Sarah's womb." He took account
of all the facts, but, looking to the promise of
God, he did not waver or doubt. Abraham
believed God.

Still more wonderful was his faith in obeying
the divine command to offer up Isaac in sacrifice. And here again it was without wavering;
for he judged that the child who had been
given to him when he himself was "as good
as dead," God could restore to him even from
death.

Much has been said and written about these tests and trials of Abraham's faith, but we seldom hear of his first great surrender, which led to all the rest. A prince among men, one of this world's nobles, he was called to abandon his splendid citizenship in what was then regarded as " the leading city of the world," and to go out to live the life of a wandering Arab. It was not that his faith seized upon the promise of an inheritance in the land of Canaan, for that promise came as the reward of his faith in obeying the divine command.[1] " He went out, not knowing whither he went." Nor was his leaving Ur a flight from a doomed city, like Lot's going out of Sodom, for it was open to him to return.[2] The secret of his faith is told us; " he looked for the city which hath the foundations, whose builder and maker is God."

" The city which hath the foundations " : these words direct our thoughts to the Apocalypse —that great stock-taking book of all the out-standing promises of Holy Writ—and there we read of the city with its foundations of price-less gems, its gates of pearl and streets of gold, with the glory of God to lighten it.

The " all " of the thirteenth verse is not

[1] Gen. xii. 7.

[2] Heb. xi. 15. Respecting Abraham's position in Ur I would refer to Colonel Conder's *Critics and the Law.*

Abraham's posterity, but the men of faith of
ancient days, who, like Abraham, desired that
heavenly country. Of these it is that the words
are written, "God is not ashamed to be called
their God." And this because of the response
their faith returned to the promises which God
had given them. The sceptic sneers at other-
worldliness; and the sneer is well deserved in
the case of any who, while claiming the heavenly
citizenship, fail to lead the sober and righteous
and godly life on earth. These old truths
need to be remembered in days like these,
when the fear of God is little thought of.
Every Christian has a Saviour, but who among
us realises what it means to have a GOD!

If these pages were intended as a homily,
much might be written about Isaac, one of
the blameless characters of Scripture. Still
more about Jacob, a mean and cunning schemer
until God, having broken his stubborn will and
won his wayward heart, linked His name with
his, proclaiming Himself the God of Jacob for
all time. About Joseph, too, whose lovely
personality is so prominent in the story of the
chosen race.

And then comes the wonderful story of Moses
who, "accounting the reproach of Christ greater
riches than the treasures of Egypt," "refused to
be called the son of Pharaoh's daughter"; and thus

relinquishing his chances of succeeding to the throne of the Pharaohs, chose the path of affliction with the suffering people of God. This, the crisis of his life, is almost forgotten in the endless controversy as to whether it dated from the Exodus, or from his flight to the land of Midian. The question surely could never have arisen but for the seeming conflict between the language of the Pentateuch and of Hebrews. Exodus tells us that the king " sought to slay him " for killing the Egyptian, and that he " fled from the face of Pharaoh." And this is supposed to clash with the words of the Epistle, that " he forsook Egypt, not fearing the wrath of the king." But the author of Hebrews was no stranger to the Exodus story, and any one who is accustomed to deal with problems of evidence will recognise that the words that seem to conflict with that story were written with definite reference to it. The Apostle declares emphatically that, whatever his danger may have been, the decisive element in his leaving Egypt was not his fear of the king's wrath, but his deliberate purpose to renounce his princely rank and to throw in his lot with the people of God. Hence the words *"By faith* he forsook Egypt "—words that have no meaning in any other reading of the passage.

" The goodness and severity of God ! " we may

well exclaim in reading that life story; for
this man, who had given up all for God, when
provoked beyond endurance by that fickle
and yet obstinate people, in a fit of petulant
anger was betrayed into forgetting what was due
to God, and thus forfeited in a moment the
prize of his whole life's work. If the story
of his life ended with the Pentateuch we might
well wish to act like that servant in the parable,
who laid up his talent in a napkin, refusing
the risks of service under such a master. But
on the Mount of the Transfiguration we see
Moses sharing in the kingdom glory of the Son
of Man. His sin was flagrant and open, and
the penalty was publicly enforced. But God,
who is abundant in mercy, having thus proved
His severity in punishing His servant's dis-
obedience, displayed His goodness by calling
him up to "the recompense of the reward"—
resurrection life, and glory.

And now let us mark yet another illustration
of the wonderful ways of God. "The time
would fail me," the Apostle exclaims, "to tell
of Gideon and Barak and Samson and Jephthae;
of David also, and Samuel and the prophets."
The sacred crypt is full, and these mighty
heroes of faith, each one of whom might claim
a special mausoleum, must rest beneath a
common epitaph. And yet, beside the memo-

rial which records the faith triumphs of him who was the greatest figure in Old Testament story, there is still a vacant space, where room can be found for one more monument, but only one. Whose name then shall be singled out for an honour so exceptional, so unique? The thirty-first verse of the chapter supplies the answer: "By faith the harlot Rahab perished not with them that believed not, when she had received the spies with peace."

Rahab the harlot! Those who seek for proofs of the divine authorship of Scripture may find one here. Was there ever an Israelite who would have thought of preferring that woman's name to the names of David and Samuel and the prophets, and of coupling it with the name of the great apostle and prophet of the Jewish faith, "whom the Lord knew face to face," and to whom He spake "as a man speaketh unto his friend!" And what Jew would have dared to give expression to such a thought? But God's thoughts are not as our thoughts. And He who immortalised the devotion of the widow who threw her last two mites into the Temple treasury, has decreed that the faith of Rahab who, like Moses, took sides with the people of God, shall never be forgotten.

And there are humble saints on earth to-day, living the Christian life, perhaps in city slums near by, or it may be in far-off heathen kraals, whose farthing gifts are as precious to the Lord as the princely offerings of men whose praise is in all the churches. [1]

---

[1] To deal with verses 39 and 40 of Hebrews xi. would need a separate chapter : here I can only offer a few suggestions. I cannot accept the usual exegesis of the words. It seems to me incredible that in any Scripture, and especially in Hebrews, *the spiritual, heavenly blessings* of the Old Testament saints should be said to depend in any sense upon " us," no matter how the " us " be interpreted. I myself would interpret it from the standpoint of the Epistle (see p. 7, *ante*). The Old Testament saints had " great and precious promises " that are common to all the people of God. But here it is *the* promise, which I take to be Abraham's special promise. He is the father of all that believe, but his distinctive promise was that he should be " heir of the world," and " a father of many nations " (Rom. iv. 13 ; Gen. xvii. 4) ; his land being the rallying centre for the nations—" the land of the promise " (Heb. xi. 9, *Gr.*) ; and his city the Metropolis of the world—" the city which hath the foundations " (Heb. xi. 10, R.V.). If Hebrews is to have a definite dispensational application to that elect " remnant " of Israel to whom pertain the bridal relationship and glory, this would afford a clue to the signification of the words " that they without us should not be made complete." But probably these words are to be explained by the fact that their resurrection awaits the fulfilment of 1 Cor. xv. 51, 52, in which we of this dispensation shall share.

11

TRIUMPHS OF FAITH

As we read the lives of patriarchs and prophets we are filled with wonder at the triumphs faith achieved in that twilight age, and we ask ourselves whether it be possible for us, who rejoice in the noontide of the Christian revelation, to rise to any higher level. What then shall we say about the "others" of whom the closing verses of the chapter speak? For of them it is that the words are written, "Of whom the world was not worthy"—humble saints many of them, whose very names are lost to us, but who are credited in heaven with still grander triumphs.

"And what shall I more say? for the time would fail me to tell of Gideon, and of Barak, and of Samson, and of Jephthae; of David also, and Samuel, and of the prophets; who through faith subdued kingdoms, wrought righteousness, obtained promises, stopped the mouths of lions, quenched the violence of fire, escaped the edge of the sword, out of weakness were made strong, waxed valiant in fight, turned to flight the armies of the aliens.

Women received their dead raised to life again: and *others* were tortured, not accepting deliverance, that they might obtain a better resurrection: and *others* had trial of cruel mockings and scourgings, yea, moreover, of bonds and imprisonment: they were stoned, they were sawn asunder, were tempted, were slain with the sword: they wandered about in sheepskins and goatskins, being destitute, afflicted, tormented; (of whom the world was not worthy); they wandered in deserts, and in mountains, and in dens and caves of the earth." [1]

Within the era of sacred Hebrew history the periods of deepest gloom were lightened by prophetic testimony, for the prophets were accredited ambassadors of heaven. And yet there were intervals during which there was "no open vision"—times when the twilight of that age was darkened by clouds that covered all the sky. And throughout the centuries between the last of the Hebrew prophets and the preaching of the Baptist, the silence of heaven was unbroken. And in those times of deepest gloom it was that faith achieved some of its noblest victories. For the faith that suffers is greater than the faith that can boast an open triumph.

---

[1] Heb. xi. 32-38.

And has this no voice for us to-day? Is it not deplorable that in the full light of the Christian revelation, we "before whose eyes Jesus Christ was openly set forth crucified,"[1] should crave for spirit manifestations, or even for subjective experiences, to confirm the truth of the promises of God? And yet tidings reach us from all lands that earnest and spiritual Christians are being deluded, and thrown into a frenzy of exultation, by the meaningless mutterings of what is called the "gift of tongues," or by other proofs of a spiritual presence from the unseen world. It is a perilous characteristic of our times. During last century there were many religious movements of this character, and there was not one of them that did not end in disaster. If real spiritual power, bringing ecstatic joy and peace to its votaries, could accredit a religious movement as divine, the Irvingite apostasy had credentials incomparably superior to any that can be appealed to by similar revivals to-day.

The story of that movement is as pathetic as it is solemn. Its leaders were eminent both as men and as Christians, no feather-headed fanatics, but staid and well-known Englishmen—lawyers, merchants, bankers, &c. They were accustomed to meet for prayer in the early

---

[1] Gal. iii. 1.

morning, not in twos and threes, but in hundreds. And the authentic records of the movement tell us of the deep peace and ecstatic joy they experienced when, seemingly in answer to their yearning prayers for Pentecostal blessing, "the power fell on them," and signs and wonders awed them—gifts of tongues, gifts of prophecy, gifts of healing.

It behoves us to profit by these lessons of the past. "Experience keeps a dear school, yet fools will learn in no other." But Christians are called upon to walk "not as fools, but as wise"; and wisdom consists in "understanding what the will of the Lord is." And the supreme purpose of God is the exaltation of Christ; "that in all things *He* might have the preeminence." The cult of the Spirit, therefore, is a departure from the line of that divine purpose, and its votaries fall an easy prey to the "seducing spirits" of the latter days.[1]

The intelligent observer of what is passing in Christendom to-day may find tokens clear and many that the lists are preparing for the great predicted struggle of the latter days between the old apostasy and the new—the religious apostasy of the Professing Church, claiming to be the oracle of God, and the infidel apostasy which, though pandering for a time

[1] 1 Tim. iv. 1.

to that venerable superstition, will eventually turn against it. And in the development of this final apostasy Satan will energise evil men, and accredit them with "all power and signs and lying wonders." " For there shall arise false Christs and false prophets and shall show great signs and wonders, insomuch that if it were possible they shall deceive the very elect."[1]

These awfully solemn words of Christ are ignored by the vast majority of Christians. And yet the signs are many that Satan is preparing the way for this his last great master-stroke. To this end the Professing Church has been leavened by one of the profanest heresies of all the ages—that in certain vitally important portions of His teaching, the Lord of Glory was the blind dupe of Jewish super-stition and ignorance and error. And the "old Serpent " of Eden further deludes men by hiding behind the mythical monster of ancient Baby-lonian paganism ; and by teaching them that demons are base and filthy creatures who help that bogie devil to degrade mankind.[1] But

---

[1] Matt. xxiv. 24.

[1] The Gospels indicate that some demons were of this type, and exercised a brutalising influence upon their victims. But they were a distinct class. The disciples could cast out other demons, but as to "this kind," the Lord told them, they were dependent on prayer to God (Mark ix. 29). If *akathartos* implied *moral* pollution demoniacs would not have been allowed to enter the synagogue, and not even the Lord's bitterest enemy would have charged Him with having a demon.

the real Satan—the Satan of Scripture—is the
god of this world, the corrupter, not of morals,
but of faith.   And the real demons are the same
that embarrassed the Lord by their homage ;
for, we read, " the unclean spirits *whensoever
they beheld Him* fell down before Him and
cried saying, Thou art the Son of God." [1]

And these are the seducing spirits of the
latter times, that we are warned against in
Scripture.   Their influence is plainly seen in
the revival of Theosophy and Spiritualism, and
in the rise of " Christian Science," " the New
Theology," and " Millennial Dawnism."   True
it is that all these movements deny the Lord
Jesus Christ ; but the mysterious fact that
demons confessed Him when He appeared on
earth is no proof that they would confess Him
in these days when the advent of the false
Christ is drawing near.   And yet, in order
to delude the Christian, they may confess Him
still.

This it was that deceived the great and
good men who were the leaders in the Irvingite
revival : how then are their imitators of to-day
to escape the snare ?   The answer will be found
in the opening words of Hebrews xii.   The
emphatic " wherefore " that begins the chapter
links up all that has gone before in enforcing

[1] Mark iii. 11, R.V.

the exhortation to "lay aside every weight and the sin that doth so easily beset us." Every weight—all that holds us back; and the easily encompassing sin—the sin of unbelief, the special sin of the Epistle to the Hebrews. And it is a sin which has no more subtle phase than that of "tempting God" by claiming proofs and tokens of His power and presence. Athletes may sometimes value stimulants, but to turn aside to seek for them is not the way to win a race! And if God should deign to grant us "Pentecostal gifts," and the "frames and feelings" which they may excite, let us receive them with grateful hearts. But to speak of "claiming" them is to give up faith for sight. Our part is to run the race that is *set before us*, and to run it "with patience," not petulantly craving for spiritual stimulants, but looking to Him who has trod the same path of unfaltering trust. "Looking unto Jesus," not here as our great High-priest, nor yet as the Son of God, nor even as the Son of Man, but as *the man* who was in all points tried as we are.[1]

The importance of the subject has led to

[1] In all the Epistles of the Apostle Paul there are but sixteen passages in which the Lord is named "Jesus," and in each of these there is either a special emphasis, or a doctrinal significance, in the use of the name of His humiliation. But Christians speak and write about the Lord of Glory just as euphony or whim may suggest. On this subject, and also as regards the significance of the title Son of Man, the author would refer to His book, *The Lord from Heaven.*

this departure from the main scheme of these pages. And indeed the character of the closing chapters forbids a strict adherence to that scheme, for they contain passages which claim special notice, although they have no special relation to the types. Such, for example, is the passage beginning with the fifth verse of chapter xii. The closely allied words here rendered chasten, chastise, correct, relate primarily to the parental training of a child. But such discipline often leads to punishment; and so *paideuo* came to have that meaning, and it is so used in Luke xxiii. 16 and 22. But our A.V., by importing that meaning into verse eight of this twelfth chapter, has led to the popular perversion of the entire passage.

With the Oriental the word "son" was not a mere synonym for child.[1] It connoted a position which was denied to a man's illegitimate offspring. But it is absurd to suppose that such children had immunity from punishment. Of *chastisement* they would probably have had more than their share, but what they did not receive was *chastening* — the kindly nurture and discipline of the parental home. The practical importance of the distinction is very great. For many Christian lives are saddened, and not a few are embittered, by

---

[1] See Chap. ii. of *The Lord from Heaven*, published by Kregel Publications, 1978.

the belief that our trials and sorrows are " chastisements," and therefore betoken divine displeasure. And there is no more cruel or mischievous phase of this error than the doctrine which is being assiduously taught in many quarters, that sickness is a proof of sin. Some of the truest and purest and holiest of His people are among the greatest sufferers from physical infirmities.

The reference to Esau, which follows in chapter xii., is generally either neglected or mis-read. It is intended as a warning, not to world-lings, but to the Hebrew Christians to whom the whole Epistle is addressed. Do both the descriptive words here used of him refer to the same crisis in his life, when for a single meal he sold his birthright ? This is a disputed point. But as the words which immediately follow relate to that one act of profanity, the introduction of any other element would seem to weaken their force. For the solemnity of the Christian life is the great lesson that the passage is meant to teach. It was " his own birthright " that Esau bartered for a passing sensual gratification—not a hope of something he might have gained, but a place that was assured to him. His " profanity " consisted in putting so vile a price on the great position which God had actually granted him. And every Christian who has a real spiritual history will appreciate the warning. For the blessing always goes with the birthright. The true effort of the Christian life is not to attain "the calling wherewith we are called," but to walk worthy of it.[1]

And the passage which follows the Esau warning reminds us of the solemnities of that calling, solemnities incomparably greater and more awe-inspiring than those of Sinai. And the recital of these solemnities leads to a repetition of that other warning with which the second chapter opens. A warning which is specially addressed to the Christian. For the "escape" here intended is not from the "eternal destruction" which will be the doom of all who shall be arraigned before the "Great White Throne," but points to that other Judgment-seat before which the redeemed must stand, and to "the Father's" judgment now and here.[1]

There are few passages more needed to-day, and few that are more misunderstood. For while the old theology tends to minimise and obscure the great truth that eternal life is the gift of God, assured to all who believe in the Lord Jesus Christ, the theology of the revival— exulting in that truth, and recognising that, as

---

[1] Eph. iv. 1.
[1] See 2 Cor. v. 8–11 (the passage must be read in the R.V.), and 1 Pet. i. 17.

regards the supreme issue of life or death, the believer " shall not come into the judgment "— is prone to belittle the reality of " the judgment-seat of Christ," and the solemnity of the Christian's life on earth in view of that judgment.

The concluding words of the chapter are intended, not to lessen the Christian's confidence, " which hath great recompense of reward," [1] but to deepen his reverence for God. They are addressed to us as " receiving a kingdom which cannot be moved." And this is the basis of the exhortation which follows : " Let us have grace whereby we may serve God acceptably with reverence and awe, for our God is a consuming fire." The reference is to the God of Sinai,[2] but it is as *our* God that we know Him.[3]

---

[1] Chap. x. 35.

[2] Exod. xxiv. 17 ; Deut. iv. 24.

[3] As so much has been written upon verses 22-24, they have been here passed by unnoticed. Two points, however, claim attention. It is strange that any Protestant expositor should accept the view that " the church of the first-born " is the Professing Church of Christendom. Indeed it is amazing in the case of such a writer as Dean Alford who has such clear thoughts, and uses such plain words, about that superstition : see *ex. gr.* his exposition of Matt. xii. 43-45, quoted on p. 83, *ante.* The New Testament references to the Professing Church of this dispensation are mainly by way of warnings of its apostasy. Were it not for the added clause, " the spirits of just men made perfect," no one perhaps would question that " the church of the first-born ones enrolled in heaven" means the whole company of the redeemed. And if that clause be held to bar such a view, the only tenable alternative is the spiritual unity of the body of Christ, which is in a peculiar sense " *the* Church."

Again, " the blood of Abel " is commonly taken as his own blood

---

crying for vengeance. But "better" is not the comparative of *bad*, but of *good*. The reference is clearly to the blood of Abel's sacrifice (see chap. xi. 4), as compared with the blood of Christ, which that and every other sacrifice prefigured. Alford's note is, "than Abel (not than that of Abel; for in chap. xi. 4 it is Abel himself who speaks, in his blood"). Of course "the blood of sprinkling" is explained by the type of Exod. xxiv. 8, which found its fulfilment in the blood of the New Covenant.

12

HEAVENLY REALITIES

As already urged, the thirteenth chapter of Hebrews is probably the "letter in few words" to which the twenty-second verse refers. This has been discussed in a preceding page.[1] No careful reader can fail to notice that here the epistolary style becomes more marked. And warnings such as those of the opening verses against immorality and covetousness appear for the first time. For the distinctive sin with which the Epistle deals is unbelief, and unbelief of the type that savours of apostasy, a going back to Judaism by those who had accepted Christ as the fulfilment of that divine religion. And to that special sin the writer reverts at the seventh verse, a fact which indicates that the change of style does not imply a change of authorship.

The "therefores" and "wherefores" of Hebrews are important as giving a clew to the writer's "argument." And the thirteenth verse of this chapter will guide us to the purpose and meaning of the verses which precede it. The clause

---

[1] See p. 12, *ante*.

begins by exhorting the Hebrew Christians
to imitate the faith of those who, in the past,
had been "over them in the Lord,"[1] and
had ministered the Word among them. Their
strength and stay, whether in life or in death,
was to be found in Him to whom pertained
the divine title of *the Same*,[2] and who,
"yesterday and to-day and for ever," fulfils
the promise of that name. Let them not be
carried away then by teachings foreign[3] to that
faith. It is good that the heart be established
by grace and not by religion.[4]

Let us keep in view that the practical
"objective" here is the exhortation "Let us
go forth unto Him without the camp, bearing
His reproach"; for His having suffered "without
the gate" was a brand of infamy. And leading
up to this, the Apostle appeals to a typical
ordinance of their religion, which was as well
known to the humblest peasant as to the
anointed priest—that none could partake of
the great sacrifice of the Day of Atonement, the
blood of which was carried by the high-priest

---

[1] 1 Thess. v. 12.   [2] Chap. i. 12 ; Ps. cii. 27.

[3] ξένος. *Cf.* chap. xi. 9. Canaan was a *foreign* country to the
patriarchs.

[4] To take the word "meats" literally is a strange exegesis ; as
though any sane person could imagine that food taken into the
stomach could establish the heart ! By a well-known figure of
speech the word "meats" is here used to represent the religion of
"the first tabernacle," which, as chap. ix. 8, 10 (to which this passage
clearly refers) tells us, stood in *meats* and drinks, &c.

into the holy place. So also is there an aspect
of the sacrifice of Christ in which His people
can have no share. But, as He exclaimed in
one of the great Messianic Psalms, " Reproach
hath broken my heart." [1] Shall His people
then claim salvation through the Cross and yet
refuse to share the reproach of the Cross? It
was the *religious* world that crucified Him—
the divine religion in its apostasy. And the
magnificent shrine that was the centre and outward emblem of that religion was still standing.
That temple was rich in holy memories and
glorious truth: how natural then it was for
them to turn to it. The Apostle had already
reminded them that if the patriarchs had been
mindful of all they had abandoned, they might
have had opportunity to have returned.[2] But
they were looking for " the city which hath the
foundations." And so it was with the Hebrew
Christians. The " way back " was ever open
to them: it was their special snare. And
therefore it was not a single act of renunciation
that he here enjoined upon them, but the constant attitude and habit of the life—an habitual
" going forth unto Him." [3] " For here (he adds)
we have not an abiding city, but we seek after
the city which is to come."

---

[1] Ps. lxix. 20.   [2] Chap. xi. 15, 16.
[3] The tense of the verb indicates this.

The whole passage then may be explained as follows. We know that, in one great aspect of His death, Christ stood absolutely alone and apart from His people. But the Cross does not speak only of the curse of God upon sin, it expresses the reproach of men, poured out without measure upon Him who was the sin-bearer. We cannot share the Cross in its godward aspect; but let us, all the more, be eager to share it in its aspect toward the world. "Let us go forth unto Him without the camp, bearing His reproach." It is the Hebrews version of the Apostle's words in Galatians vi. 14, "God forbid that I should glory, save in the cross of our Lord Jesus Christ, by whom the world is crucified unto me, and I unto the world."

The words "without the camp" have a two-fold significance. For no Hebrew Christian would miss their reference to the apostasy of the golden calf. The thirty-third chapter of Exodus records that, because of that apostasy, God rejected Israel. This we learn from the fifth verse. And then, we read, "Moses took the tabernacle, and pitched it without the camp, afar off from the camp, and called it the tabernacle of the congregation. And it came to pass, that every one which sought the Lord went out unto the tabernacle of the congrega-

tion, which was without the camp." [1] Save for
the apostasy within the camp, an Israelite who
" sought the Lord without the camp" would
himself have apostatised. But when the people
rejected God by setting up an idol, He refused
any longer to acknowledge them, until they
were restored to favour by the intercession of
Moses. And when, because of the unspeakably
more awful apostasy of the crucifixion, Israel
ceased to be " the congregation of the Lord,"
it behoved the disciple to take sides with Christ,
who "suffered without the gate."

But here the Apostle reverts to the wilderness
typology on which the teaching of the whole
Epistle is based; and instead of the *city*, he
speaks of the *camp*. "Let us go forth unto
Him without the city," would have implied
that when the Lord was crucified His people
ought to have forsaken Jerusalem, whereas the
Lord expressly enjoined upon them to tarry

---

[1] This was not *the* tabernacle. But it is an ignorant exegesis to
suppose that it was merely a meeting-place for the devout. The
words " the tabernacle of the congregation," made so familiar to us by
our A.V., must be read " the tent of meeting." The phrase occurs
for the first time in Exod. xxvii. 21, and the references there given in
R.V. margin (chap. xxv. 22 ; xxix. 42; xxx. 36) prove that it meant
the place where God would meet those who sought Him. It was
the designation given to the sanctuary divinely ordered in xxv. 8; and
it is so used repeatedly in the four following chapters. The statement,
therefore, that Moses gave this title to the tent he pitched without
the camp is clear proof that that tent was provisionally appointed as
the tabernacle, the erection of which was no doubt delayed by the
apostasy of the golden calf.

there; and even when the Church was scattered
by the Stephen persecution, the Apostles still
remained in the holy city.

All this is of great practical importance in
our applying this passage of Hebrews to ourselves. And though no part of the Epistle
ought to appeal with greater force to the
Christian, its teaching is almost wholly lost.
Not only so, but it is often so perverted as to
become a defence of error which the Epistle
was written to refute. Indeed the commonly
received exegesis of these verses in itself affords
a justification of Hengstenberg's dictum, that
the doctrine of the types has been "entirely
neglected" by theologians. The "we" and the
"they" of verse ten are emphasised in order
to support the figment that we Christians have
an altar of which Jewish priests had no right
to eat. For nothing but the presence of very
emphatic pronouns could warrant an exegesis
so entirely foreign to the whole spirit of the
Epistle. And yet, in fact, there are no pronouns at all in the text! For, as we have seen,
the Apostle is not enunciating a new truth
of the Christian faith, but referring to a familiar
ordinance of the Jewish religion.

There is a general agreement that the verse
refers to the type of the great sin-offering of
the Day of Atonement. But here agreement

merges in a controversy as to whether the altar of sin-offering has its antitype in the Cross of Christ, or in Christ Himself. And those who maintain that the Cross is the altar of sin-offering urge that it was there, " outside the camp," that Christ " offered Himself " as the great sin-offering. But, as a matter of fact, Scripture knows nothing of an altar of sin-offering ! And further, not even that great annual sin-offering was killed upon the altar. It was killed " by the side of the altar before the Lord." [1]   And seeing that, excepting the fat which was burned upon the altar, the entire carcase was burned without the camp, the figment that we Christians may eat of our great sin-offering is in flagrant opposition to the teaching of the type. But, worse far than this, it is a direct denial of the truth which the type is here used to illustrate, namely, that in the great sin-offering aspect of it His people can have no part in the sacrifice of Christ: " Alone He bore the Cross."

Most expositors who advocate the somewhat conflicting readings of the verse above noticed, are too intelligent not to see that the word altar

---

[1] As Lev. xvi. contains no explicit direction as to this, I assume that it was killed in the same place as the ordinary sin-offerings, namely, beside the altar (for such is the meaning of the words " on the side of the altar "). The only sin-offering ever killed outside the camp was the red heifer of Numb. xix. (see p. 36, *ante*).

is here used in a figurative sense. Confusion
and error become hopeless with those who take
it literally, and apply it to the Lord's Table.
For this not only involves all that is erroneous
in the rival views above indicated, but it is
inconsistent both with the typology of the
Pentateuch, and with the doctrinal teaching of
the New Testament. The redemption sacrifices
of Exodus, and the various sacrifices of the
law enumerated in the other books of Moses,
are each and all intended to teach different
aspects of the work of Christ in all its divine
fulness. And therefore, if the types be neglected,
our theology is apt to be defective. Of the
two main schools of Protestant theology, for
example, the one gives such undue prominence
to the teaching of the passover that in certain
respects it ignores the teaching of the sin-
offering; while the other gives an almost exclusive prominence to the sin-offering, forgetting
that the Leviticus sacrifices were for a people
who had been already redeemed and brought
into covenant relation with God by the great
sacrifices of Exodus.

And this error lends itself to the further
error of supposing that a sacrifice necessarily
implies an altar. There was no altar in Egypt,
and yet "the house of bondage" was the
scene of the first great sacrifice of Israel's

redemption. And as the Israelites ate of the sacrifice on the night of their deliverance from Egypt, so also on every anniversary of that night there was a memorial celebration of their redemption, when they met in household groups, without either altar or priest, to partake of the paschal lamb. And at the paschal supper it was that the Supper of the Lord was instituted —a fact the significance of which would be plain to a Hebrew Christian. For the Lord's Supper bears the same relation to the redemption accomplished at Calvary that the paschal supper bore to the redemption accomplished in Egypt. [1]

Let us then keep clearly in mind that the paschal supper was not a repetition, but only a memorial, of the great redemption passover. For, unlike the many sacrifices of the law, these redemption sacrifices were *never to be repeated*, but were offered once for all. *Sacrifices*, I say, for, as we have seen, the sacrifice by which the covenant was dedicated pointed back to the paschal lamb, and the blood of the covenant was the complement, so to speak, of the blood of the passover. Hence the words with which at the Supper the Lord gave the Cup to the disciples: "This is my blood of the New Covenant." [2] The conclusion is thus confirmed that it is

---

[1] See Appendix I.   [2] Matt. xxvi. 28.

the death of Christ as the fulfilment of the *redemption* sacrifices that the Supper commemorates.

However we approach the subject, therefore, it is clear that to speak of an altar or a priest in connection with the Lord's Supper has no Scriptural sanction. These errors of the religion of Christendom would have revolted the Hebrew Christians. Their special snare was a clinging to the religion of type and shadow which pointed to Christ, and which was fulfilled at His coming. But the errors of Christendom bespeak an apostasy which savours of paganism. For, except in the spiritual sense in which every Christian is a priest, an earthly priest outside the family of Aaron must be a pagan priest, and an altar save on Mount Moriah must be a pagan altar. When the Lord declared that Jerusalem would cease to be the divinely appointed place of worship upon earth, it was not that Christianity would set up "special sanctuaries" (I quote Bishop Lightfoot's phrase once more), but that the true worshippers should "worship the Father in spirit and in truth."[1]

And surely we can sympathise with the feelings of a Hebrew Christian as, standing in the Temple courts thronged with worshippers at the hour of the daily sacrifice, he watched the divinely

---

[1] John iv. 23. See p. 76, *ante*.

appointed priests accomplishing the divinely
ordered service which, during all the ages of his
nation's history, had been the most ennobling
influence in the national life.   Every element of pious emotion, of national sentiment—
of superstition, if you will—must have combined
to attract and fascinate him, as with reverence
and awe he gazed upon that splendid shrine
which had been raised by divine command
upon the very spot which their Jehovah God
had chosen for His sanctuary, the place where
kings and prophets and generation after generation of holy Israelites had worshipped for more
than a thousand years.   With such thoughts
and memories as these filling mind and heart,
nothing but the revelation of something higher
and more glorious could ever wean him from
his devotion to the national religion.

With what indignation and contempt he
would have spurned the altars and the priests
of the religion of Christendom!   But the
Epistle to the Hebrews sought to teach him
that as a partaker of a heavenly calling, he
had to do with heavenly realities, of which
the glories of his national cult were but types
and shadows.   As a pious Jew he did not need
to learn the truth which even paganism knows,
though the sham " Christian religion " is ignorant
of it, that the place for the altar and the

priest must be the place of the worshipper's approach to God. While therefore Israel, being an *earthly* people, had " a sanctuary of this world," the place of worship of the heavenly people was to be the presence of God in heaven.

13

HIS FULL PROVISION

" Be not high-minded, but fear." This apostolic
warning, addressed to us Gentiles, is entirely
in keeping with the Lord's parable of the Great
Supper.[1] But both parable and precept are
ignored in Christendom. And yet the parable
might suggest a further thought. Street waifs
and wayside tramps are fully satisfied if only
they can find " bit and sup " and keep clear of
the police. And most Christians are very like
them in this respect. For, misapplying that other
apostolic precept, " Having food and covering, let
us be therewith content," they have no spiritual
ambitions beyond obtaining forgiveness of sins
and immunity from " the wrath to come." If
our salvation is assured, what more can we
need ? It is not strange, therefore, that such a
book as Hebrews is neglected ; for its purpose
is not to tell how sinners can be saved, but to
unfold the infinite fulness there is in Christ
for sinners who have obtained salvation. Therefore it is that the passover has no place, and the
sin-offering but a secondary place, in its doctrinal
teaching.

[1] See p. 55, *ante.*

In seeking to call attention to neglected truths, repetition is unavoidable. The Israelites, as we have seen, were "saved" ere they raised their triumph song on the wilderness shore of the sea. But a man's release from a criminal charge gives neither right nor fitness to enter the king's palace; and this parable may serve to exemplify Israel's condition when gathered round Mount Sinai. The doom and bondage of Egypt they were for ever done with, but they had neither fitness nor right to approach the Divine Majesty. And if the Pentateuchal narrative ran differently, and we read there that God gave the law in order that His people might thereby attain to holiness, and thus gain access to His presence, the record would have accurately prefigured our popular theology upon this subject. But in emphatic contrast with this we find that before they set out on their wilderness journey their redemption was completed by the great covenant sacrifice. By the sprinkling of the blood of the covenant they were sanctified; and the law with all its elaborate ritual was designed, not as a means by which they might attain to holiness, but as a gracious provision to maintain them in all the blessing which was theirs by virtue of the covenant.

The true effort of the Christian life is not to become what we are not, but to live worthily of what God in His infinite grace has made us in Christ. In the Epistles of the New Testament, therefore, the characteristic and most usual designation of Christians is "saints," or holy people. But the truth being lost that the Christian is not only justified, but sanctified by the blood of Christ, this scriptural name for Christians is now treated as a purely conventional expression, and it is practically obsolete.[1] The standard of Christian living has thus been lowered. And just in proportion as the great type which prefigured this aspect of the work of Christ drops out of view,[2] the Epistle to the Hebrews is misunderstood. For it supplies the key to its doctrinal teaching.

The great covenant sacrifice is, as we have seen, the note struck in the opening clause

---

[1] The words "saint" and "holy" in our English Bible represent but one word in the original. And as the apostate church has degraded our word "saint," it is a pity that in the sixty odd occurrences of it we do not read "holy people." The change would remind Christians of their "calling."

[2] The Christian is not only justified but sanctified by the blood of Christ (Rom. v. 9; Heb. xiii, 12). In 1 Cor. i. 30 we have these truths stated apart from typical language, though with a plain reference to the types. We there read that Christ is "made unto us both righteousness and sanctification, even redemption." Redemption in its fulness as including all that was prefigured by both the twelfth and the twenty-fourth chapters of Exodus. But this is obscured in our versions, neither of which translates the "both," plain though it is in the Greek; and thus the epexegetical force of the "and" is lost. Theology teaches that while we are righteous in Christ, holiness must be attained through the work of the Holy Spirit. Scripture teaches that holiness of life, like righteousness of life, is a practical conformity to what we are in Christ. And this is what the Spirit's work signifies.

of chapter one. That note vibrates throughout the Epistle,[1] and in its concluding sentences it rings out loud and clear: " Now the God of peace, who brought again from the dead the great Shepherd of the sheep in virtue of the blood of the eternal covenant, even our Lord Jesus, make you perfect in every good thing to do His will, working in you that which is well-pleasing in His sight through Jesus Christ; to whom be the glory for ever and ever. Amen."

This reference to the Resurrection is framed upon the Pentateuchal narrative, but the actual words are taken from the Septuagint version of Isaiah lxiii. 11, which reads: " Where is He that brought up out of the sea the Shepherd of the sheep?" And here, as in the only other mention of the Resurrection in Hebrews (chap. i. 5 and 6), the Ascension is regarded as the complement and completion of the exaltation of Christ from the grave to the throne. The marginal rendering of the earlier passage is now generally accepted: " When He bringeth again the first begotten into the world, He saith, And let all the angels of God worship Him." The reference to the Resurrection is clear, the only alternative being the strange suggestion that the homage of angels is

---

[1] See *ex. gr.*, chap. viii ; ix. 12, 19, 20 ; x. 29 ; xii. 18–21.

deferred until the future advent. Some distinguished expositors adopt that suggestion, but this weighs nothing as against the explicit statement of Scripture. For we are expressly told that at the Ascension He was proclaimed the King of Glory (Ps. xxiv. 7–10). And reading the heavenly visions of the Apocalypse in the light of such prophecies and of His prayer on the betrayal night (John xvii. 5), we rejoice to know that all the heavenly host now worship Him as enthroned in heaven.

It is noteworthy that while the words "And let all the angels of God worship Him" agree substantially with Psalm xcvii. 7 in the Greek Bible, they are letter for letter identical with Deuteronomy xxxii. 43, as given in that version. True it is that our "Received Text" contains nothing corresponding to them; but we must not forget that the authors of that version had Hebrew MSS. more than 1000 years older than any we now possess. And moreover the Epistle to the Hebrews is Holy Scripture, the writing of an inspired Apostle.

"The God of peace": to take these words as a veiled rebuke aimed at supposed divisions among the Hebrew Christians, is to lose the significance of this most gracious climax to

the teaching of the Epistle. Christians generally have two Gods—the God of Sinai,
and the God revealed in Christ. But "*our*
God is a consuming fire"[1]—the same God
Who declared Himself at Sinai.[2] The work
of Christ has not changed either His nature
or His attributes; but it has made it possible
for Him to change His attitude toward sinful
men. We have seen how clearly this is
unfolded in the typical story of Israel at
Sinai before and after the covenant sacrifice
was offered.[3] And just as in virtue of that
covenant "the great and terrible God" of
Sinai could dwell among His people, so in
virtue of the New Covenant God can declare
Himself as "the God of Peace," and bid
us to draw near to Him, and to draw near
with boldness.

"With boldness," because we have such a
full redemption, and such a Great Priest in
the heavenly sanctuary which is our place of
access. But this is not all. For here on earth
we are a flock without a fold,[4] and we are
conscious of our weakness and our proneness
to wander. And to meet these our needs we

---

[1] Heb. xii. 29.   [2] Exod. xxiv. 17.

[3] Exod. xix. 21–25; xxiv. 9–11; xxv. 8.   See p. 112, *ante*.

[4] On John x. 16 Dean Alford writes: "Not one fold, as erroneously
rendered in A.V., but one flock; no exclusive enclosure of an outward
Church."

have a shepherd. It was a marvellous triumph of faith that before Christ came His people could believe in a *personal* God and make words such as those of the twenty-third Psalm their own. With what fulness of meaning and of joy ought we as Christians to be able to claim them now! For "in virtue of the blood of the eternal covenant" our Lord Jesus is "the great Shepherd of the sheep."

But even this is not all. For we are not merely "the sheep of His pasture," but morally responsible human beings. And we are living in a world where God is not owned, and in circumstances that are uncongenial to the Christian life. And His purpose for us is, not that we should spend "the time of our sojourning here" in failure and sin, with intervals of penitence, marked by abject cries for mercy, but that we should consistently live to His praise, as becomes those who have such a salvation and such a God. Every divinely inspired prayer in Holy Scripture expresses what God is willing and ready to do for His people. And here is the closing prayer of this most blessed and wonderful Epistle: "Now the God of peace . . . make you perfect in every good thing to do His will, working in you that which is well-pleasing in His sight."

"Is that you, darling?" We all know the pathetic story, and how the other child, who was not the "darling," sadly answered, "No, mother, it's only me." And with too many Christians "it's only me" expresses the response the heart makes to His appeal to them to follow Him as His "beloved children."[1] That Enoch *pleased* God is the Greek Bible rendering of the Hebrew words that he "walked with God." And both are joined in the Apostle's exhortation: "how ye ought to walk and to please God."[2] But such a standard of Christian life, even for a single day, is deemed visionary and unpractical. We are "only me" Christians.

"Make you perfect"; it is a different word from that which is thus rendered in other passages in the Epistle.[3] It means primarily to restore or put in full order again,[4] and secondarily to equip or to furnish completely.[5] To set us tasks beyond our powers and yet to hold us responsible for failure would be worthy of an oriental savage. This is not God's way. His call to service ensures a full provision to enable us to do His will. And it is not a

---

[1] Eph. v. 1.   [2] 1 Thess. iv. 1.

[3] *Katartizō* occurs again in x. 5 and xi. 3 ("framed").

[4] As in Gal. vi. 1.

[5] As in 1 Thess. iii. 10, and 1 Pet. v. 10. The kindred word used in 2 Tim. iii. 16 is used of fitting out a ship.

question of benefits peculiar to some of His
people, but of His purpose and desire for all.
The perfecting, therefore, is not by means of
exceptional spiritual gifts, but through the
Lord Himself. " To Whom be the glory
for ever and ever."

" Suffer the word of exhortation ": " Our
brother Timothy is set at liberty ": " Salute
all your leaders." How delightful are these
human touches in the Divine Scriptures! We
are thus reminded that the words we have
been considering are not the rhapsody of a
" saint " in the sense ecclesiastical,[1] but the
sober utterances of one who, though an inspired
Apostle, and the greatest of all the Apostles,
was the most intensely human of men. And
as we read " the word of exhortation " we
think, not of " saint " Paul, with a halo round
his head, as raised to a pinnacle which ordinary
Christians cannot be supposed to reach, but
of him who " obtained mercy " in order that
he might be " a pattern " to believers like
ourselves.[2] And we seem to hear him say to
us: " I beseech you, brethren, be ye followers

---

[1] With what indignation the Apostle would spurn a title denied to
all the holy martyrs who have been butchered by the Church from
which this " honour " comes, but accorded to many evil men (like
" Saint " Cyril of Alexandria, and certain of the Popes, and many
other sham " saints " of Christendom! Joan of Arc is the latest
addition to the galaxy).

[2] 1 Tim. i. 16.

of me—be ye followers of me, even as I also am of Christ." [1]

"Salute your (spiritual) leaders." At the one end of the ecclesiastical gamut of Christendom we have sacrificing priests, and at the other extreme all ministers are systematically denied a formal or definite recognition. The one is sheer paganism, the other is chargeable with ignoring or belittling the Lord's provision of ministers until the end (Eph. iv. 11–13). The foundation of Apostles and Prophets remains, but the "building of the body of Christ" is the work of evangelists, pastors, and teachers, and to ignore them is to dishonour Him Whose gifts they are.

For it is not a question here of "spiritual gifts" in the 1 Corinthians sense, but of men who are themselves the gifts of our ascended Lord. And there is no vagueness in the way they are mentioned. For they were to be obeyed, and a special greeting was sent to them. "Obey your leaders," "salute your leaders" would be quite unmeaning if the persons designated were not definitely known. And the explicitness of the mention of these shepherds is increased by the context which speaks of "the Great Shepherd." The relation

------

[1] 1 Cor. iv. 16; xi. 1.

of pastor and flock is but little recognised
to-day, but it is a holy bond, and altogether
divine; for it depends on the Lord's gracious
provision, the continuance of which is assured
until all ministry is merged in its glorious
consummation.[1]

The primary meaning of the verb translated
"them that have the rule" in Hebrews xiii. 7,
17, 24 (*hēgeomai*) is to lead or go before, and
then to be a leader, to rule. It is a word
of such elastic meaning that in the first of its
twenty-eight occurrences it is rendered *governor*
(Matt. xi. 6), and in many passages, *think, count,
reckon, esteem* (as in 1 Thess. v. 13).

The Apostle's use of it, especially in this last
cited instance, clearly suggests that in Hebrews
xiii. he employs the word in its primary sense.
The "leaders" here, therefore, were not their
official rulers, but their spiritual guides who
ministered the Word of God among them.
There was probably no need for such an
exhortation in the case of men apostolically
appointed to office in the Church. Indeed the
tendency to give undue honour to the *episkopoi*
culminated in the grossly profane homage
claimed for them in the *pseudo* - Ignatian
epistles.[2] I call them *episkopoi* because (as

---

[1] Eph. iv. 8–13.

[2] The authorship of the epistles is matter of controversy. The evidence points to Callistus, who was elected to the papacy a century

Dean Alford bluntly says in his Commentary on 1 Timothy), "the *episkopoi* of the New Testament have officially nothing in common with our bishops." Though some *episkopoi* did "labour in the word and teaching,"— and such were to be held in special honour —they were appointed, not to teach, but to rule.[1]

No less true is it that the *diakonoi* of the New Testament have nothing in common with our "deacons." As an exception to this, indeed, the service for the "making of deacons" preserves the ordinary New Testament meaning of the word, and New Testament truth about ministry. For before ordaining a candidate the bishop requires from him an assurance that he is divinely called to the ministry—"truly called according to the will of the Lord Jesus Christ." What the Apostle said of his own

---

after the death of Ignatius. His prospects were prejudiced by his having been a slave, a criminal, and a convict. But by representing that the saintly Ignatius had had similar antecedents he turned the prejudice round in his favour. That a man with such a past should have been Bishop of Antioch in the early days of truth and purity is most improbable. Still more improbable is it that Ignatius could have written such epistles. Here is a typical passage:—" It is good to recognise God and the Bishop. He that honoureth the Bishop is honoured of God. He that doeth aught without the knowledge of the Bishop, rendereth service to the devil." Profane drivel of this kind was possibly acceptable to the leaders of the Roman Church in the age of Callistus. These words are not written in ignorance of Bishop Lightfoot's treatise on the subject.

[1] 1 Tim. v. 17.

ministry — that it was neither by man nor
through man—is true of every real minister
of Christ. Ordination is but the Church's
recognition of the divine call.

The distinction between *diakonoi* and *episkopoi*—ministry and office—appears from Scriptures such, *ex. gr.*, as Philippians i. 1, and
1 Timothy iii. 8–10. These passages give further
proof that the ministers of the Word were as
definitely known as the office-bearers, although
(as appears from 1 Timothy iii. 10) they were
not appointed in the same way. The Apostle's
injunctions were explicit : " Let them first be
proved, and, being found blameless (not, let
them be ordained, but) let them minister." The
phrase " use the office of a deacon " is a sheer
mistranslation for ecclesiastical reasons. For
our word *deacon* has no precise equivalent in
the Greek language. *Diakonos* is used of household servants (as in John xi. 5, 9), of " Ministers
of the Word," of Apostles, and even of the
Lord Himself (Rom. xv. 8).

In Ephesians iv. 8–13 the Apostle speaks of
the Church as the vital unity—the body of
Christ. In 1 Corinthians xii. 28–31 he is speaking of " the visible church," the organised
society on earth. In Ephesians iv., therefore,
there is no mention of " governments " or of
" gifts " in the First Corinthians sense. And

as the ministry of evangelists is not exercised within the Church, but in the world without, they are not mentioned in 1 Corinthians xii. 28.[1]

---

[1] As the administration of the Professing Church is admittedly not conducted now on New Testament lines, there is room here for differences among Christians ; but the fact that in Apostolic times Ministers, in the spiritual sense, were never formally *appointed*, destroys every excuse for refusing or failing to accord them definite recognition in any community claiming to be Christian.

I should add that there is no scriptural warrant for applying the word *deacon* in a special sense to the Seven of Acts vi. 5. And (as Dr. Hatch clearly shows) the duties assigned to them pertained to the Eldership, when the Church was fully constituted.

14

CHRISTIANITY IS CHRIST

"THE catacombs are full of Christ. It was to Him that the Christians of the age of persecution ever turned: it was on Him they rested —in gladness and in sorrow; in sickness and in health; in the days of danger—and these were sadly numerous in the first two centuries and a half—and in the hour of death. It was from His words they drew their strength. In the consciousness of His ever-presence in their midst, they gladly suffered for His sake. With His name on their lips they died fearlessly, joyfully passing into the Valley of the veiled Shadow. On the tablet of marble or plaster which closed up the narrow shelf in the catacomb corridor where their poor remains were reverently, lovingly laid, the dear name of Jesus was often painted or carved."

"If we believe . . . that our Lord founded a visible Church, and that this Church with her creed and Scriptures, ministry and sacraments, is the instrument which He has given us to use, our course is clear. We must devote our energies to making the Church adequate to the Divine intention—as strong in principle, as broad in spirit as our Lord intended her to be; trusting that, in proportion as her true motherhood is realised, her children will find their peace within her bosom. We cannot believe that there is any religious need which at the last resort the resources of the Church are inadequate to meet."

The first of these quotations is from the Dean of Gloucester's *Early Christians in Rome:* the second is from Bishop Gore's *Mission of the Church.* And they are brought together here to exemplify in a striking way the contrast between the faith of Christ and the religion of Christendom.

In Christianity the Lord Jesus Christ is all and in all. But in this system Christ is an institution to be administered by the Church. Professor Harnack puts it with epigrammatic force: "Christ as a person is forgotten. The fundamental questions of salvation are not answered by reference to Him; and in life the baptized has to depend on means which exist partly alongside, partly independent of Him, or merely wear His badge." Ministers of Christ are the *Church's* ministry: the Lord's Supper is *her* sacrament; and

even the Divine Scriptures which speak of
Him are *her* Scriptures, bracketed with *her*
creed as being of equal authority and value.

What are our needs in the spiritual sphere?
Forgiveness of sins?—the Church will grant us
absolution.   Peace with God?—we shall find it
in the Church's "bosom."   Grace to help in
time of need?   Comfort in sorrow?   Strength
for the struggles of life, and support in the
solemn hour of death?   The whole burden of
our need "the resources of the Church" are
adequate to meet.

And "the Church" of this scheme, as
we are expressly told, is the "visible Church,"
and the visible Church as writers of this
school understand it.   It is not the true
spiritual Church, the vital unity of the Body
of Christ, nor even "the Holy Catholic
Church" as defined by the Reformers, but the
Professing Church on earth, the "outward
frame," as Alford calls it, now drifting to its
"fearful end." [1]

How true it is that where vital truth is in-
volved there is no clear line of demarcation
between what is unchristian and what is antichristian.   And nothing but the after-glow of
lost truth and the piety of a devout spirit

---

[1] See p. 83, *ante*.   On the Reformers' teaching about "The visible
Church," see Appendix IV., *post*.

separates this evil system from the goal to which it legitimately leads.[1]

If the above cited words expressed merely the views of the school to which their author belongs, they would not deserve notice here. But they are a development of the false teaching of the Fathers, as epitomised by Dr. Hatch in the sentences from his Bampton Lectures quoted in my first chapter. Hence their bearing on the thesis of that chapter, and on my present subject. Is it strange that men whose minds were warped by such error should seek, by denying the apostolic authorship of Hebrews, to disparage an Epistle in which the Church and " her sacraments " are never mentioned?

Not that Hebrews is peculiar in this respect. For in Romans, the greatest doctrinal treatise of the New Testament, the very word *ekklēsia* is not to be found until we reach the characteristically " Pauline " postscript of the concluding chapter. Never once does the word occur in the writings of the Apostle Peter. Never once in the Apostle John's great doctrinal Epistle. Indeed if we except First and Second Corinthians it appears only thirty-seven times in all the Epistles. And there are not a dozen passages in the whole of the New Testament

---

[1] Those only who have lived in a Roman Catholic country can realise how evil is this system, and yet how Christian in spirit an adherent of it may be.

in which it stands for the Professing Church on earth. For though "the Church" in that sense holds such prominence in almost every phase of the religion of Christendom, the New Testament seldom refers to it save by way of warnings of its apostasy.

Overwhelming proof this that "the Church" has no such place in Christianity as that which is assigned to it in Christendom. For were it otherwise appeal would certainly have been made to its authority in all the Epistles, and very specially in every section of the Epistle to the Hebrews. Indeed, the Apostle Paul's charge to the Ephesian elders, recorded in the twentieth chapter of Acts, ought to be "an end of controversy" on this subject. If the "motherhood" and the "resources" of the Church were not antichristian error but divine truth, they would have prominent mention here. But his main allusion to "the Church" is his sadly pathetic and most solemn forecast of heresies and schisms; and in view of these impending evils and perils, he commends them to *God and the Word of His grace.*

And in keeping with the spirit of the Apostle's words I wish, in these closing pages, to use this deplorable and pernicious error merely as a dark background to throw into relief the truth which was the strength and joy of the early

Christians before the apostasy took shape. "The catacombs are full of Christ," the Dean of Gloucester repeats in the clause succeeding that above quoted from his book. He then goes on to tell that in those "first days" "the Good Shepherd" was "the favourite symbol of the Christian life and faith." And he adds: "A great and eloquent writer (Dean Stanley) does not hesitate to speak of what he terms the popular religion of the first century as the religion of 'the Good Shepherd.' He says they looked on that figure, and it conveyed to them all they wanted. And then he adds sorrowfully that 'as ages passed on, the image of the Good Shepherd faded away from the mind of the Christian world, and other emblems took the place of the once dearly loved figure.'"

Yes, in those bright days the thought of the personal and living Christ "conveyed to them all they wanted." How deep the apostasy in which this simple faith was corrupted and ultimately swamped by base superstitions about the "motherhood of the Church" and her "resources to meet every religious need." What a contrast to the inspired words of the Apostle, "My God shall supply *all your need* according to His riches in glory by *Christ Jesus!*" And *He* is "the same yesterday and to-day and for ever."

The Church is not a sheepfold, as this false system pretends.[1] The word *ekklēsia* has no such meaning in the New Testament. Indeed it had no such meaning in the Greek language when the New Testament was written. The Church is the flock, and Ministers are to be "ensamples to the flock" — the Lord's own provision of shepherds until the Chief Shepherd shall appear.[2] He is the *Chief* Shepherd with reference to the under-shepherds. He is the *Good* Shepherd, because He cares for the sheep, and gave His life for them. And as brought up again from the dead He is the *Great* Shepherd.

The significance of the imagery of the Lord's words in the tenth of John was familiar to the Hebrew Christians of Palestine,[3] but we are apt to miss it. Within the fold, sheep have no need of the shepherd's care. But when he leads them out to pasture they look to him for guidance, and they run to him for safety whenever danger threatens. What intensity of meaning this must have had for those early saints in days of persecution! "The religion

---

[1] See p. 131, *ante.*

[2] 1 Pet. v. 3. The word rendered *pastor* in Eph. iv. 11 is "shepherd," and is so translated in every other of its eighteen occurrences in the New Testament.

[3] It is noteworthy that to them were addressed the only Epistles in which the Lord is expressly named as Shepherd (1 Peter and Hebrews).

of the Good Shepherd" is indeed a beautiful
conception; and it was an evil day when that
figure was supplanted by the crucifix and the
Latin cross; and the image of a living Saviour
and Lord gave place to emblems that speak of
a dead Christ.

There were also reasons of another kind why
Hebrews was not adequately appreciated by
the Latin Fathers. In marked contrast with
the writers of the New Testament, one and all
of whom, like Timothy, had known the Holy
Scriptures from their childhood, the early theologians of the Primitive Church were converts
from paganism. While, therefore, much of
their homiletic teaching is most valuable, their
doctrinal expositions of the Old Testament are
too often untrustworthy. And the ignorance
that marks so many of their writings respecting
the typology of the Pentateuch and the divine
scheme of prophecy that permeates all the
Hebrew Scriptures, influences our theology to
the present hour.

But this was not all. Just as the modern
Jew is prejudiced against Christians on account
of the persecutions by which his people have
suffered from apostate Christianity, so in early
days the Gentile Christians were no less prejudiced against the Jews on account of their
part in instigating certain of the persecutions

to which the Church was subjected by pagan Rome. It was therefore natural, perhaps, that the Fathers should have no sympathy with Jewish hopes as revealed in Scripture, and that the unnumbered prophecies and promises relating to the restoration of Israel to divine favour should have been ignored, or else "spiritualised" to foster the false conception of "the Church," which they bequeathed as a baneful legacy to Christendom.[1] This being so, an Epistle addressed to Hebrews must have seemed an anachronism. And an Epistle written in the language of Old Testament typology must have been in great measure an enigma.

And a cavil of a somewhat similar kind is heard to-day on wholly different grounds.

Ordinary Christians are not more in bondage to the prevailing error about the visible Church on earth than are some other Christians to the truth about the Church, the Body of Christ. And because that truth has no place in Hebrews they would rob us of the Epistle. It is not that they doubt its claim to be Holy Scripture, but they urge that "it is not for *us*." It belongs, they say, to the Pentecostal dispensation which was broken off when the covenant people

---

[1] The reader has but to open a Bible at the later chapters of Isaiah, *ex. gr.*, to find by the headings of the chapters that this perversion of Scripture, begotten of ignorance and prejudice, still prevails in Protestant and Christian Britain.

were set aside, and which will be resumed when they are again restored to favour. But this betrays forgetfulness of the Apostle's words to Timothy that "all Scripture is profitable . . . that the man of God may be perfect, thoroughly furnished unto all good works."

If we are to be restricted to those portions of Scripture which are specially addressed to Christians of the present dispensation, our Bible will shrink to very narrow limits. It is *all* for us, though it savours of Gentile ignorance and pride to suppose that it *belongs* to us. The Epistle to the Romans is clear as to that. To the covenant people it was that the oracles of God were entrusted. It was because they were false to the trust that they were temporarily set aside. But as the Apostle says, their want of faith cannot make the faithfulness of God of none effect.[1] For not merely the calling but the *gifts* of God are "without repentance."

As the Bible is God's revelation to His people upon earth, it belongs in a peculiar sense to His earthly people, and we are only "tenants for life" of the inheritance; yet during our earthly sojourn our right to appropriate this priceless gift of Holy Scripture in every part of it is absolute.

---

[1] Rom. iii. 1–3, R.V.

Hebrews, moreover, is not addressed to the earthly people as such, but to an election from the covenant people, who are "partakers of a heavenly calling." And this being so we can take our place by their side, and profit to the full by the precious teaching of an Epistle which contains truth that is of vital moment to us, and truth that is found nowhere else in Scripture. For here alone we learn of the Priesthood of the Son of God for us in heaven now, securing our access to the Divine Presence.

And Hebrews supplies the clew to the typology of the Pentateuch; for it unfolds with peculiar fulness what the death of Christ imports in its manifold aspects toward both God and the sinner. And thus we learn the unity of the Bible. For in teaching that the Pentateuch is "the word of the beginning of Christ," it brings together the earliest and the latest of the divine Scriptures, and shows that all are one.

And grace permeates its teaching. For though it may not declare in the same sense as Romans does, the truth of grace upon the throne,[1] it tells

---

[1] For that is a distinctive truth of the present dispensation. All judgment is committed to the Son. But He is now sitting on the throne of God *in grace*, "exalted to be a Saviour." But when the mystery of God shall be finished, there will follow, not the bonfire, but the age of righteous rule—the times of the restitution of all things, of which all the prophets have spoken (Rev. x. 7; xi. 15; Acts iii. 19–24. See p. 87, *ante*).

of the throne of grace, to which we may come boldly that we may find grace to help in time of need. It speaks of the Spirit of grace. It warns us against falling from grace, and exhorts us to have grace whereby we may serve God acceptably. It tells of the blessedness of a heart established with grace. And "Grace be with you all" are its closing words.[1]

We cannot afford, then, to tolerate any disparagement of an Epistle which, to quote Bishop Westcott's words again, "deals in a peculiar degree with the thoughts and trials of our own times." No book of the New Testament indeed has a more special bearing upon the present-day phase of the main branches of the antichristian apostasy. For though Rome, regarded as a definite organisation, is losing ground everywhere, as a *system* it has perhaps more influence in England to-day than at any period since the Reformation. And if the voice of open infidelity is less heard in Britain now than formerly, it is because its mission is being insidiously accomplished within the Professing Church.

The leaders of the Oxford movement maintained the supreme authority of the Bible. And in following the teaching of the Fathers in this

---

[1] This is, in its most condensed form, the Apostle Paul's characteristic "benediction" at the close of every one of his fourteen Epistles. And it is found in no other Epistle of the New Testament.

respect their movement was hostile to Rome. But the "antiquity" which was their fetich was not that of "the foundation of Apostles and Prophets"—not that of the Church of the New Testament—but of the Church of the Fathers. Their appeal was to the Patristic theologians and the Œcumenical Councils. And this evil leaven has worked so efficaciously that after two generations the "National Reformed Church of England" has ceased to be Protestant, and even the great Evangelical Party is little more than a memory of the past.

For, as we have seen, the Romish conception of "the Church" is merely a development of Patristic teaching. The Reformers, perhaps out of consideration for the devotees of so venerable a superstition, dealt with it by re-definitions. But the root-error of the apostasy could not be destroyed without treatment of a far more drastic kind, and Christianity soon lapsed again to the level of a "religion." "Lapsed," I say, for the Christianity of the New Testament is not a "religion."[1] In those days the State required that all Roman subjects should profess some religion, but the Christians, who had neither altars nor priests, neither sacrifices nor images, were held to have "no religion at all," as Laud in his day said of the Scottish people; and so

---

[1] See Archbishop Trench on James i. 27 (*Synonyms*).

they were looked upon as atheists,[1] and punished accordingly; and this even by such enlightened rulers as Trajan and Marcus Aurelius. The Hebrew Christians had not changed a good religion for a better, but, as the Apostle reminded them, they had turned away from the one divine religion in accepting Him who was the fulfilment of all its typical ordinances, and the substance of every truth it had foreshadowed. CHRISTIANITY IS CHRIST. There is no truth more needed to-day than this; and no Book of Scripture teaches it more fully and explicitly than the Epistle to the Hebrews.

Referring to this false conception of "The Church," Dean Farrar writes:[2] "The whole Epistle to the Hebrews is a protest against it." And with equal force may this be said of the sceptical movement of the day. No one who reads Hebrews in the light of the Pentateuchal types could be deluded by the profane figment that the Books of Moses are literary forgeries concocted by the apostate priests of the exilic era. For the typology answers to the New Testament revelation of Christ as exactly as a key fits the lock it is intended to open.

---

[1] This is mentioned by Justin (Apol. i. 5, 16) and also by Tertullian (Apol. 10). And Eusebius records that when calling upon Polycarp to renounce his fellowship with Christians, the Proconsul used the words, "Repent: say, 'Away with the Atheists.'"

[2] *Lives of the Fathers*, ii. 603. His words have special reference to the teaching of Augustine. The whole passage is of great importance.

More than this, the adage about the trees shutting out the view of the wood is strikingly exemplified by the critics. For nothing but ignorance of the Bible as a whole can lend an air of plausibility to their " assured results." Their writings indicate that their study of Holy Scripture is purely analytical. Of its scope and purpose they seem to know nothing, and nothing of what Pusey aptly calls its " hidden harmony." The order of the revelation is plain. As Hebrews declares, the Pentateuch is " the word of the beginning of Christ." " He wrote of Me " is the Lord's description of the Books of Moses. And as countless Scriptures indicate, the Prophets belonged to a later age ; for prophecy is the divine provision for a time of apostasy.

This was the Bible on which our Divine Lord founded His Messianic Ministry. This was the Bible of the Apostles. The Bible of the Martyrs. The Bible of Christians of every name for eighteen centuries, until German Rationalists were raised up (was it by the Spirit of God, or by another spiritual power ?) to prove that in all His teaching on this subject the Lord of Glory was speaking merely as an ignorant and superstitious Jew ; and that, being Himself the dupe of the errors of Rabbinic Judaism, He enforced these errors upon His disciples by declaring again and again with extreme solemnity, that the very words in which He taught them were divinely given. Language could not be more explicit: " I have not spoken from myself, but the Father which sent me, He hath given me a commandment, what I should say, and what I should speak: . . . the things therefore that I speak, even as the Father hath said unto me, so I speak." [1]

The contemptuous answer vouchsafed to this by the critics is that " both Christ and the Apostles or writers of the New Testament held the current Jewish notions respecting the divine authority and revelation of the Old Testament." [2] Unitarianism has never challenged the teaching of Christ, but only the meaning put upon His words; but the " Higher Criticism" impiously flouts His teaching as being both ignorant and false. Nothing more daringly profane, more shameless in its blasphemy, has ever marked the evil history of the Professing Church. Some people may accept these " assured results of modern criticism " and yet continue to believe in the divine authority of Holy Scripture and the deity of Christ (the superstitious will believe anything!); but, recognising the goal to which

---

[1] John xii. 49, 50.

[2] Hastings' *Bible Dictionary*, Art. " Old Testament," p. 601. This is the standard text-book of the cult. It carries on the title-page the name of Prof. Driver of Oxford.

these " results " inevitably lead, all intelligent and thoughtful men who accept them will take refuge in Agnosticism.

Though there is no unity in error, a kinship marks its various phases. And what the inspired Apostle wrote about the " seducers " of his time [1] applies unreservedly to-day : by a true instinct the spiritual Christian rejects any heresy which touches the honour of his Lord. And the pivot upon which this most evil heresy turns is the *kenōsis* doctrine that enables pundits and Professors to sit in judgment on the teaching of the Lord of Glory. " The whole Epistle to the Hebrews is a protest against it." And even if these pages fail of their main purpose, they will not have been written in vain if they serve to rescue some, even of " the poor of the flock," from the toils of these " seducers."

---

[1] 1 John ii. 23–27.

1

THE PRIESTS OF CHRISTENDOM

SINCE penning the strictures upon the priests of Christendom, contained in some of the preceding pages, I have taken up by chance a book that I had not opened for more than thirty years. I refer to *The Doctrine of the Priesthood*, by the late Canon Carter of Clewer, a book that is accepted as an authoritative defence of the errors which it advocates. It claims to prove that those errors are in accordance with the teaching (1) of the Church of England, (2) of the Church of the Fathers, and (3) of the New Testament. No fair-minded man would deny that, with very few exceptions, the errors of the Romish system are the fruit of the evil seed of Patristic teaching. Nor can it be denied that many traces of these evil doctrines appear in the formularies of the National Church. But it has been authoritatively decided again and again that those formularies are to be construed in the light of the Articles; and the testimony of the Articles is unequivocally Protestant.

What concerns us here, however, is his appeal

to the New Testament. In the following sentences he summarises his main proofs that the ministry of the Christian Church is sacerdotal :—

"St. Paul is here (1 Cor. xiv. 16) speaking of that act of ministry to which he had alluded previously in the same Epistle, as his own habitual office; 'The cup of blessing which *we* bless, is it not the communion of the Blood of Christ?' (1 Cor. x. 16). Again, when St. Paul, writing to the Romans, dwells on the grace that is given to him as an Apostle, he uses throughout terms of Priesthood; 'that I should be the minister (λειτουργόν, lit. a Priest, so used, itself or its derivatives, Heb. viii. 2, 6; ix. 21; x. 11; St. Luke i. 23) of Jesus Christ to the Gentiles; ministering (ἱερουργοῦντα, lit. as a Priest) the Gospel of God, that the offering up (προσφορά, a sacrificial offering) of the Gentiles might be acceptable, being sanctified by the Holy Ghost' (Rom. xv. 16)" (p. 81).

This is what passes for argument and evidence with writers of this school! Let us analyse and test his statements. What a commentary upon his statement about the Apostle's "own habitual office" is supplied by such Scriptures as Acts xx. 7, and 1 Cor. iii. 5! And here I would refer to Lightfoot's words quoted on page 77, *ante*. Carter's argument from 1 Cor. x. 16 depends entirely on the emphasis he lays on the pronoun *we* (the italics are his). Will the reader believe it that there is no pronoun in the text! *Leitourgos*, he tells us, means literally a priest. But Grimm's *Lexicon* tells us that it means "a servant of the State, a minister, a servant, servants of a king, servants of a priest." And the Concordance tells us that the word occurs but five times in the New Testament. Besides Rom. xv. 16, and Heb. i. 7 and viii. 2, the Apostle uses it only of Roman magistrates who enforced the payment of taxes (Rom. xiii. 6), and of the bearer of the money and other gifts sent him by the Philippians during his imprisonment in Rome (Phil. ii. 25). *Leitourgia* is used in that same connection (Phil. ii. 30); and again in the same sense in 2 Cor. ix. 12 (service). Again in Phil. ii. 17 (service). These, with Heb. viii. 6 and ix. 21, are its only occurrences in the Epistles. The verb *leitourgeo* occurs only twice in the Epistles—viz. in Heb. x. 11 and in Rom. xv. 27 (where he enjoins on the Gentiles their duty to *minister* to the poor Jews in " carnal things "). As to *prosphora* I need but refer to pp. 33 *ff.*, *ante.* In Scripture neither offering nor killing a sacrifice was essentially a priestly function at all (see p. 35, *ante*). And Grimm's meaning for *hierourgeo* is " to be busied with sacred things, to minister in the manner of a priest." And Bengel's note upon the verse is (referring to the three words in question), " This is allegorical. Jesus is the priest; Paul the servant of the priest." Phil. ii. 17, where the Apostle speaks of his being poured out as a drink-offering, is another striking instance of an allegorical use of liturgical terms.

It is untrue that any one of these words " means " what this writer says it means—as flagrantly untrue as if he said that *doulos* means a Christian minister. It is sometimes used of Christian ministers, just as these other words are sometimes used in the sense he claims for them. But they were words in common use among Greek-speaking Gentiles; and the Christians in Rome and Corinth would naturally give them their common meaning.[1]

This last remark applies with peculiar force to another of the "proofs" to which these men attach special weight. Canon Carter writes :—

"Nor is it of little moment to our inquiry to observe that the original words translated in our version 'Do this in remembrance of Me,' had in the ears of a Jew a fixed meaning, long hallowed in the usage of the people, as connected with sacrifice. 'Do (ποιεῖτε) this,' in the language of the Septuagint, means, as it meant among heathen writers, 'offer as a sacrifice'" (p. 84).

How can we discuss such a question with any one with whom this sort of thing passes for "argument"? The question at issue is whether the Lord's Supper is a sacerdotal rite; and there is no doubt that if this were established, the very common word *poieo* might be understood in that sense, as it is often so used in the Septuagint. But will some one tell us what other word the Lord could have used? For the word is as common in Greek as is *do* in English. And though it occurs many hundreds of times in the New Testament, it is never used

---

[1] It is very noteworthy that these words were never used by the Apostles Peter or James; and that, doubtless, because their ministry was specially to the *Jewish* Christians who might have been betrayed into construing them in a wrong sense.

in a sacrificial sense. The Passover in Egypt, moreover, was not a priestly rite (see p. 27, *ante*); and the yearly paschal supper was merely a household celebration of Israel's redemption on that memorable night. There was no priestly element in it. But "learned ignorance" confounds the Supper of fourteenth Nisan with the Feast which began on the fifteenth—a blunder which lends some show of plausibility to the error of supposing that the Lord's Supper is a priestly and sacrificial rite, and leads to the further heresy of supposing that the four Gospels differ as to the events of Passion week.[1]

But to the passage last quoted Canon Carter adds :—

"So also the term 'in remembrance of Me' (εἰς τὴν ἐμὴν ἀνάμνησιν), or rather, 'for a memorial of Me,' is sacrificial; the memorial in a sacrifice being that portion of the victim which is laid on the altar and offered to God, in order to bring the whole oblation to remembrance before Him. The idea implied is not that of an act of memory on the part of man, but a memorialising of God" (p. 85).

These statements are wholly unfounded. The LXX do not use the word *anamnēsis* of "that portion of the victim which is laid on the

---

[1] See Lev. xxiii. 5, 6, and Numb. xxviii. 16, 17. "In the fourteenth day of the first month is the passover of the Lord; and in the fifteenth day of this month is the feast." The A.V. has this blunder in Matt. xxvi. 2, where the words *in the feast* are added—a blunder that is all the stranger on account of the explicit statement of the fifth verse, and also of John xiii. 1. The Last Supper was *before* the Feast. As verse 29 shows, the disciples supposed that Judas went out to buy what was needed for the feast, for trading was lawful on the night of the passover. (See Edersheim's *Life and Times of the Messiah*, ii. 508.)

altar." And the kindred word *mnēmosunon* (which occurs in Matt. xxvi. 13; Mark xiv. 9, and Acts x. 4) is never used by the LXX of a *victim* sacrifice, but only of *meal* offerings. And though it occurs in the Septuagint, *ex. gr.* in Exod. xii. 14, it there represents a different Hebrew word. And in Exod. xii. 14 it was not the paschal lamb, but the *ordinance*, that was to be a memorial. And that, not to God, but to the people. The words are explicit: "This day shall be *unto you* for a memorial."

As regards *anamnēsis* (which occurs in Luke xxii. 19; 1 Cor. xi. 24, 25, and Heb. x. 3) I will appeal, not to Protestant expositors, but to the *Lexicon*. The meaning which Grimm gives of the word is "a remembrance, recollection" (and quoting Luke xxii. 19), "to call Me (affectionately) to remembrance." And referring to Heb. x. 3 he adds, "The memory of sins committed is revived by the sacrifice."

The question here at issue, however, is not one of words merely. It is a conflict between divine truth and vital error. The Lord's Supper is thus degraded by making the elements a memorial of a dead Christ. And this, *mirabile dictu*, to bring to *God's* remembrance the death of His Son! It is the false cult of the Crucifix. This error would be impossible were it not that the words of our Divine Lord are either entirely ignored, as in the Mass, or relegated to an incidental and subordinate place, as with most Protestants. The Supper (as 1 Cor. xi. tells us) is emphatically a showing (or proclaiming)[1] of the Lord's death : but first and pre-eminently it is not a memorial of His *death*, but (as Grimm puts it) an affectionate remembrance of *Himself*, in view of His absence and His coming again. His words are explicit : "Do this in remembrance of ME"—not a dead Christ, but an absent Lord. The added words, "Ye do show the Lord's death till He come" were not uttered by the Lord Himself, but were given by Him through His inspired Apostle.

But "the Catholic Church" knows no Coming save the great day of wrath; and ignoring the living Lord, it appoints sham priests to do on earth what He is doing for us in the presence of God. It thus sets up "the first tabernacle again," which is a denial that the way into the holiest is open (Heb. ix. 8). And this again is a denial of the efficacy of the blood of Christ, and of the redemption He has wrought. This cult of the Crucifix is not merely unchristian but antichristian.

The "Holy Catholic Church" claims to be the oracle of God, and therefore it requires from its votaries an unreasoning acceptance of its dogmas. Protestantism, on the other hand, appeals to Scripture and reason in support of the doctrines for which it claims belief. But the attempt to defend Romish errors by Protestant methods is not only futile but foolish.

---

[1] The word is usually rendered "preach," as in 1 Cor. ii. 1; ix. 14, &c.

2

THE DOCTRINE OF THE BLOOD

THAT strange phase of teaching about "the blood of Christ," of which Bengel is the most distinguished of modern exponents, cannot be ignored in studying Hebrews. His treatise on this subject on Heb. xii. in the "Gnomon of the New Testament" is painful reading to most of us. He argues that "not even a drop" of the Saviour's blood remained in His body: and that His blood after being shed was free from all corruption (Peter i. 18, 19). And among his further theses are the following:—"It cannot be affirmed that the blood which was shed was again put into the veins of the Lord's body." "At the time of the Ascension the blood separated from the body was carried into heaven." And "the blood of Jesus Christ always remains blood shed." Under this thesis he says: "The condition of the blood shed is perpetual. Jesus Himself is in heaven, and His body is also there; so too is His blood in heaven; but His blood is not now in His body." This material blood was sprinkled upon the mercy-seat in heaven; and if I understand Bengel aright, the sprinkling is repeated from time to time, as in the case of the Leviticus type.

To understand Christian truth, I once again repeat, we need to know the language in which it has been revealed. And that language is supplied by the divine religion of Old Testament typology. Bengel's appeal, therefore, to Patristic authority counts for nothing; for the Fathers neglected the study of that language, and their "blood" theology was leavened by the doctrines and practices of the cults of classic paganism (see p. 147, *ante*). The pagan doctrine of washing in blood, so abhorrent to Judaism and so utterly foreign to Christianity,[1] was the counterpart of the pagan figment that water could wash the soul from sin. In Scripture washing is always and only with water. And when used in a doctrinal sense the figure means clearing ourselves in a practical way from evil. When, *ex. gr.*, Ananias said to Paul, "Wash away thy sins," he was using a figure which any Jew would understand: "Arise and be baptized, and turn away from your past evil life." And the Apostle's words to the Corinthians, "You washed yourselves" (1 Cor. vi. 11) had precisely the same meaning.

But "the water of purification" of Numb. xix. owed its typical efficacy to having flowed over the ashes of the sin-offering; and when

---

[1] The revised text of Rev. i. 5 (*luō* for louō) is now accepted. *The Gospel and Its Ministry*, chap. xiv., notices every passage which bears upon this question. The blood bath was a well-known pagan rite.

sprinkled on the sinner it renewed to him the
benefits of the sacrifice. And the sprinkling
of the blood is to be interpreted in the same
way. The Israelite thus obtained the benefits
of a sacrifice accomplished.

If Christ had re-entered heaven in virtue of
His Deity, He must have stood apart from His
people. But having entered there in virtue of
His blood—that is, of the death by which He put
away sin—He is there by a title that He can
share with His people. Therefore is it that He
is the mercy-seat—the meeting-place between
God and men. Twice only does this word
occur in the New Testament: in Heb. ix. 5 it
refers to the typical "propitiatory," and in Rom.
iii. 25 to Christ Himself, the antitype. To
suppose, as Bengel's theory implies, that there is
a coffer of some sort in heaven on which Christ
sprinkles His material blood, is a vagary of
exegesis which is as deplorable as it is amazing.

The truth or error of that exegesis is easily
tested. "Almost all things are by the law
purged with blood": that is, by having sacrificial blood sprinkled upon them. Now this
blood-sprinkling must have the same significance
in every case. Nothing that we deem holy can
be sanctified save by the reality—whatever it
be—intended by that figure. But let us confine
ourselves here to the two great types above
mentioned. We are redeemed by the reality
typified by the sprinkled blood of the paschal
lamb, and sanctified by the sprinkled blood of the

covenant sacrifice (Exod. xii. and xxiv.). Does this mean that "the material blood of Christ is sprinkled upon us sinful men?" The question has only to be stated to expose its error. We are redeemed and sanctified when we receive by faith in Christ the "merits" of His death for us.

"The blood is all one with the life" (Lev. xvii. 14, R.V.). Blood shed, therefore, typifies life laid down and lost. In plain words "blood" is a figurative expression symbolising *death*. But if, as Bengel holds, "blood" is to be taken literally in Heb. xiii. 20, it must be so construed also in x. 19. And if the material blood of Christ be meant in ix. 12, it must have the same meaning in verse 14. That passage is specially important. The words of verse 12 are, "Neither by the blood of goats and calves, but by His own blood, He entered in once for all into the holy place, *having obtained eternal redemption.*" It is not the Priest going in to make atonement —to finish an unfinished work—but the Mediator going in on the ground of a work finished and complete. It has been overlooked that the types of Lev. xvi. and Exod. xxiv. are blended in verse 12, and that the prominence is given, not to the sin-offering, but to the "calves and goats" (see verse 19) of the covenant sacrifice (see p. 18, *ante*). When Moses went up to God in Exod. xxiv., he entered the Divine presence by (διά) the blood, as really as Aaron did when he passed within the veil. For no other way of approach is possible.

3

THE "PAROUSIA"

OF the twenty-four occurrences of the word παρουσία in the New Testament, six relate either to Stephanus, Titus, or the Apostle Paul; and it is used once in relation to "the man of sin" (2 Thess. ii. 9); and once to "the day of God" (2 Pet. iii. 12). The following are the sixteen passages in which it relates to Christ: Matt. xxiv. 3, 27, 37, 39; 1 Cor. xv. 23; 1 Thess. ii. 19; iii. 13; iv. 15; v. 23; 2 Thess. ii. 1, 8; James v. 7, 8; 2 Pet. i. 16; iii. 4; 1 John ii. 28.

The meaning of the word, according to Grimm's *Lexicon* is, "1st, presence; 2nd, the presence of one coming; hence the coming, arrival, advent. . . In the N. T., especially of *the advent*, *i.e.* the future, visible *return* from heaven of Jesus, the Messiah, to raise the dead, hold the last judgment, and set up formally and gloriously the Kingdom of God."

The *parousia* is thus deferred till "the end of all things," whereas in fact it is matter of controversy, whether the word is used in that sense

in any of the sixteen passages above specified.
And let no one suppose that this is merely a
question of accuracy in the use of words, or
that it has no importance save in relation to
eschatology. The truth, and therefore the
divine authorship of Holy Scripture are in-
volved, as plainly appears from the writings of
"Meyer and others, who hold that the *Gospel*
prophecies are inconsistent in their eschatology
with those after the ascension, and again with
the chiliastic ones of the Apocalypse" (Alford
on Matt. xxiv.). Certain it is indeed that if
the conventional doctrine of the advent be
right, the prophecies on the subject are hope-
lessly at variance. But Scripture is divine, and
its harmony is perfect.

The earliest prophecies of the Coming were
the Eden promise of the woman's seed (Gen.
iii. 15) and the Enoch warning of judgment
(Jude 14). And in after ages many a further
prophecy was added—some that spoke of redemption to be accomplished by a suffering
Messiah, others that foretold the blessedness
and glory of His righteous rule, and others
again of which the burden was judgment. In
interpreting these Scriptures the Jew forgot
that they were the word of Him with whom
a thousand years are as one day. And the
theology of Christendom, unwarned by the
errors of Jewish exegesis, subtracts all that
have been fulfilled at "the first advent," and
throws all the rest into hotchpotch (as the

lawyers would say), together with the additional prophecies of the New Testament; and the resulting mass of irreconcilable predictions is blindly referred to what is called "the second advent."

All the more inexcusable this, because there are distinctive prophecies in the New Testament which are not the counterpart of anything revealed in the Hebrew Scriptures. For the divine scheme of prophecy relating to earth, as unfolded in the Old Testament, has definite reference to the covenant people; and their rejection of Christ seemed to thwart its fulfilment. But the sins of men cannot thwart the purposes of God; and their apostasy led to the revelation of a wider purpose which had been "kept secret since the world began." And the contemplation of the wonders of that revelation led the Apostle who received it to exclaim, "O the depth of the riches both of the wisdom and knowledge of God! how unsearchable are His judgments and His ways past finding out!" (Rom. xi. 33).

That revelation contains three distinctive "mysteries," namely, the Gospel of Grace; the Church, the Body of Christ; and that "Coming" which will be the consummation of this dispensation of Grace and of the Body.[1]

---

[1] The word "mystery" in the Epistles does not mean a puzzle, but a secret. Dr. Sanday explains it as " something which up to the time of the Apostles had remained secret, but had then been made known by divine intervention."

Though "Grace came by Jesus Christ," it
was veiled during His earthly ministry. But
when sin reached its climax the only possible
alternatives were "the doom of Sodom or the
mercy of the Gospel"—judgment unmixed, or
grace unlimited. And grace prevailed. God
committed all judgment to the Lord Jesus
Christ, and He, the only Being in the universe
who can judge a sinner, is now seated on the
throne of God as *a Saviour*. It is not merely
that there is grace for all who come to God
through Him, but that grace is reigning. The
divine moral government of the world is not in
abeyance, but all judicial or punitive action
against sin is deferred (2 Pet. ii. 9). The
great amnesty has been proclaimed. God is
not imputing unto men their trespasses, but
beseeching them to come within the recon-
ciliation (2 Cor. v. 19, 20).

We must not confound the gospel of Rom.
i. 1 with that of Rom. xvi. 25—the gospel
which God "promised before by His prophets
in the Holy Scriptures," and the gospel which
was specially revealed to and through the
Apostle Paul. "*My* gospel," he calls it, "even
the preaching of Jesus Christ, according to the
revelation of the mystery which was kept secret
since the world began, but now is made manifest, and by prophetic Scriptures . . . made
known to all nations." Grace was plainly
foreshadowed in the "evangelical" Hebrew
prophets; but the truth of grace *enthroned*

was a "mystery" (or secret) revealed after the rejection of the covenant people.[1]

Meanwhile, as a consequence of that rejection, the main stream of Messianic prophecy (which always runs in the channel of Hebrew history) is tided back. What then of the election from Israel, who have accepted Christ during the nation's rejection of Him—"We who have pre-trusted in Christ," are the Apostle's words (Eph. i. 12)?

The answer is given in the Epistle to the Ephesians: they are raised to a position of heavenly blessing and glory as the Body of Christ—a truth that is entirely outside the scope of the Old Testament Scriptures. But the "mystery of Christ" includes more than this; for Gentile believers, instead of being relegated to the position of proselytes, are now "fellow-heirs and fellow-members of the Body" (Eph. iii. 3–6, R.V.).

We have seen, however, that the grand scheme of Messianic prophecy relating to earth, though now in suspense, is in no way abrogated. It is therefore obvious to the intelligent student of Scripture that before it can be resumed the present "economy" must be brought to a close. But how? and when? The "when" is entirely

---

[1] This, and not the truth of "the body of Christ," is the "mystery" that is to be "made known to all nations." The rendering, "the Scriptures of the prophets" in verse 26 is a mistranslation which erroneously connects the passage with the opening words of the Epistle. The "prophetic writings" of xvi. 26 are those of the New Testament.

with God, and all chronological forecasts are greatly to be deprecated. But the "how" is plainly told us in the Apostle's well-known words which reveal the third distinctive "secret" of the Christian revelation:—"Behold, I tell you a mystery: We shall not all sleep, but we shall all be changed, in a moment, in the twinkling of an eye, at the last trump: for the trumpet shall sound, and the dead shall be raised incorruptible, and we shall be changed" (1 Cor. xv. 51, 52).

This is "the Coming of the Lord" of which the Apostle speaks by express revelation in 1 Thess. iv. 15–17. As Dean Alford says in his note upon the passage, the word "first" in verse 16 relates to the "then" of verse 17, and "has no reference whatever to the *first resurrection*" (Rev. xx. 5, 6). And referring to 1 Thess. iv. in his note on 1 Cor. xv. 52, he says the trumpet there mentioned is "the last trump in a wide and popular sense." Indeed the thought of a general resurrection of all the dead at the same time is quite unknown to Scripture.

Lord Bacon's scheme for what he calls "history of prophecy" is still a desideratum, and it is specially needed in this sphere. It is, he says, "that every prophecy of Scripture be sorted with the event fulfilling the same throughout the ages of the world." And any one who will take up the inquiry will find in the pursuit of it, as Bacon says, "a confirmation of faith." For the study will throw light upon the ground-plan of the Bible, to systematised ignorance of which is mainly due the success of the sceptical crusade of the sham "Higher Criticism." And the seeming conflict between the various *parousia* prophecies of the different books of the New Testament is due to the want of this "sorting." For example, to speak of "the second advent," to "set up the kingdom and hold the last judgment," betrays ignorance of the fact so plainly revealed that these events will be separated by at least 1000 years. And if, as some maintain, the 1000 years are not to be taken literally, the period may extend far beyond a "millennium."

This subject would fill a volume; a few brief suggestions must here suffice. At the Ascension, while the disciples stood round the Lord upon the Mount of Olives, "a cloud received Him out of their sight." And two heavenly messengers promptly brought them the promise that He would "so come in like manner" as they had seen Him go into heaven (Acts i. 9–11). Now this was plainly a confirmation of the prophecy of Zech. xiv. 4, and it is wholly distinct from the "Coming" of 1 Thess. iv., as this again is distinct from the "Coming" of 2 Thess. ii. 8, which may perhaps be identical with that of Rev. i. 7; though even here we must not dogmatise, for the manifestations of Christ will be many. And whether any one of these "Comings" be the same as those fore-

told by the Lord in the Gospels is matter
for inquiry. They may all be closely related
chronologically, or they may be separated by
prolonged intervals of time. Ignorance alone
will dogmatise on this subject. For, as Pusey
says, " Prophecy was not given to enable us
to prophesy, but to be a witness to God."

There is no element of chronology, however,
in relation to that Coming which is to bring
this episodical " Christian dispensation " to a
close. " The apostolic age maintained that
which ought to be the attitude of all ages, constant expectation of the Lord's return " (Dean
Alford on 1 Tim. vi. 14). In a preceding page
an explanation of the delay in its fulfilment
has been suggested. And indications are not
wanting that even now the stage is preparing
for the resumption of the long-suspended drama
of Israel's national history. But there is no
event that *must* occur, no line of prophecy
that *must* be fulfilled, before the realisation of
what Bengel rightly calls the forgotten hope
of the Church.[1]

Some who value this truth create a prejudice
against it by the use of unscriptural phrases,
such *ex. gr.* as " the secret rapture "; " the
Lord's Coming for His Church," &c. &c. We
are not told that the Coming which is to bring
this dispensation to a close will be secret. Nor

---

[1] It has been urged that, as the Apostle Peter knew he was to die,
and the Apostle Paul knew he was to visit Rome, the Coming was
not a present hope in Apostolic times. To call this quibbling would
be discourteous.

is there any Scriptural warrant for supposing
that the resurrection pertaining to it may not
include all the holy dead from Abel downwards.
Again, to speak of the Lord's "coming back
to earth *with* His Church" is no less unwar-
ranted. And in the absence of definite Scripture
we may well refuse to believe that the children
of *grace* of the present dispensation will have
any share in the Lord's ministry of vengeance.
May not the "saints" with whom He will
return to execute judgment be "His holy
myriads" of the angelic host?

It may be said, perhaps, that phrases such
as those here deprecated express legitimate inferences from Scripture. But in this sphere no
inferences are legitimate. "If I will that he
tarry till I come, what is that to thee?" was
the Lord's answer to Peter's inquiry about his
brother Apostle. And the disciples at once
inferred that "that disciple should not die."
What other inference could they draw? But,
as the record adds, the Lord did not say "he
shall not die," and His actual words are repeated with emphasis (John xxi. 20–23). All
the more striking this, because the Pentecostal
proclamation indicates that a national repentance
would have brought the fulfilment of the Old
Testament Messianic prophecies of the kingdom
(see p. 87, *ante*).

Our part is not to draw inferences from the
Scriptures which speak of His Comings, but,
as Bacon phrases it, to *sort* them. And let

us begin by grasping the elementary truth that
" God has not cast away His people whom
He foreknew," and that *in relation to earth*
Israel will be the centre of His action in all the
various phases of the *parousia*. How many
such phases there will be is matter, not for
dogmatism, but for reverent inquiry. Another
of Bacon's pregnant words will here be opportune.
He speaks of " divine prophecies, being of the
nature of their Author with whom a thousand
years are but as one day." Divine Scripture,
like divine philosophy, is " not harsh and crabbed,
as [people of a certain sort] suppose." But the
plain fact is that the conventional theory of
" the second advent " is based on what Charles
Kingsley somewhere calls " our covert atheism "
in refusing to believe in any direct divine inter-
ference with this world of ours prior to the final
crash of all things. The open atheist is more
intelligent when he points to the absence of
divine action, in support of his unbelief. But
the silence of God in this dispensation is explained by the " mystery " of Grace enthroned.

4

THE VISIBLE CHURCH

" THE visible Church of Christ is a congregation of faithful men in the which the pure word of God is preached, and the sacraments be duly administered according to Christ's ordinance in all those things that of necessity are requisite to the same."—(Article XIX.)

In the *Churchman's Theological Dictionary*[1] Canon Eden states the different views taken of the phrase, " the visible Church," in this sentence ; and then, after noticing the fact " that there is no such thing on earth as the Catholic Church existing as one community," he suggests that perhaps the writer, " through mere oversight, translated *Ecclesia Christi visibilis, the* Church, when the evident meaning is *a* Church."

But if this phrase be in itself ambiguous, the fact of Cranmer's authorship of the Article removes all doubt as to its meaning.   And in the rest of the sentence there is no ambiguity whatever.   It is not " the " but *a* (*i.e.* any) congregation of faithful men."   And to make this still more explicit it goes on to exclude

---

[1] Revised edition, (p. 87) with a commendatory " Introductory Notice," by the Principal of Ridley Hall (now Bishop of Durham).

the Greek and Roman Churches from the category of visible churches of Christ, thus vetoing the figment that the corporate position of blessing depends upon an historic sequence.[1] Wherever "the pure Word of God is preached, and the sacraments are duly administered according to Christ's ordinance"—there is "a visible Church of Christ." But where the Word of God is corrupted or discredited, or where Christian baptism and the Lord's Supper are ousted by baptismal regeneration and the Mass, such a congregation, whether it be a Chapel or a Parish Church, is outside the pale.

In the case of the Reformers the "Church's motherhood" declared itself by butchering the saints of God, and among "her resources to meet every religious need" were the torture chamber and the stake. And men who *bought* the truth at a terrible cost were not the men to *sell* it (Prov. xxiii. 23). But in these days the truth costs us nothing, and we are ready to barter it for plausible errors and venerable superstitions, in order to maintain a false peace and the semblance of unity.

To quote the Archbishops' decision in the Incense case, "It was the purpose of the then rulers of the Church to put prominently forward the supremacy of the Bible." The conception of the Church which the Reformers thus repudiated is the root error of the apostasy. If that error be accepted, great and devout

---

[1] No one enslaved by that error could have written Article XXIII.

thinkers like J. H. Newman are prepared to believe the "blasphemous fable" of transubstantiation.[1] And men who are not incarnate devils, but devout and kind-hearted human beings, will condone and approve the Church's cruelties and crimes. "For no means came amiss to it, sword or stake, torture chamber, or assassin's dagger. The effects of the Church's working were seen in . . . the hideous crimes committed in His name" (Froude's *Council of Trent*).

But, we shall be told, these crimes were the work of the Apostate Church in evil days now past. Yes, but what concerns us here is that if we accept the traditional, antcihristian conception of "the Church,"[2] they are not crimes at all. Moreover, as Froude so wisely says, "the principles on which it persecuted it still professes, and persecution will grow again as naturally and necessarily as a seed in a congenial soil." And *ex hyp.* the Romanisers are right in denouncing the Reformation as itself a "hideous crime"; and nothing but Protestant ignorance and British pride will make us adhere to the Churches of the Reformation, or the more modern organisations of Revival times.

---

[1] Article XXXI. Cardinal Newman's words are, " I had no difficulty in believing it as soon as I believed that the Catholic Roman Church was the oracle of God, and that she had declared this doctrine to be of the original revelation."

[2] It is incredible that any one holding that view could have written the Homily on the Church (Article XXXV.).

" The Church to teach " : how harmless and right it seems. And yet it is the germ of the error which (as Article XX. clearly shows) the Reformers meant to kill by insisting on the supremacy of the Bible, and claiming for the Christian the right to appeal to it, even against the teaching of the Church.

Moreover, the Church is " a congregation of faithful men," not a college of teachers set over them. It is not the shepherds but the flock. " Every particular or national Church " necessarily possesses powers of a certain kind, but such powers are strictly limited (Article XXXIV.). And no " particular or national Church " is *the* Church. " Christ's Holy Catholic Church " the Reformers defined to be " the whole congregation of Christian people dispersed throughout the whole world." [1] What grand Christians those Reformers were !

And if the Reformation is becoming a spent force in this country, it is because modern Evangelicalism is enervated by the Romish conception of " the Church." " Which is the true Church ? " This utterly false question accounts for every secession to Rome. And Evangelicalism no longer gives in bold plain words the answer the Reformers gave, [2] that no body on earth is " the Church " in the sense implied in the question. But Latin theology entirely ignores the failure of the Professing

---

[1] The fifty-fifth Canon of the Convention of 1603.
[2] See p. 178, *ante*.

Church on earth,[1] confounding it, as it always does, with the unity of the Body of Christ. And further, it always takes words spoken by the Lord to His Apostles *as such*, as though they were addressed to the Church of Christendom.

" Who cares anything for any church save as an instrument of Christian good ! " If all true Christians were animated by these bold words of Chalmers—one of the greatest " churchmen " of the nineteenth century—and if they thought less of their Church and more of their Lord, true spiritual unity would become a reality in the sight of all men.

---

[1] As a matter of accuracy it may be noticed that the habitually used phrase " the Church of Christ " is never found in Scripture, though " Churches of Christ " sometimes occurs, i.e. *congregations.* " The Church of God " is the scriptural title given to the Church on earth in its primitive purity. Eph. and Col. deal with the Spiritual Church, the Body of Christ ; 1 Cor. xii. and xiv. and 1 Tim. iii. give us what the New Testament has to say about the " outward frame " of the Professing Church on earth. For " the visible Church " has no such place in Scripture as it holds in the theology of Christendom.

SCRIPTURE INDEX